Stacy

Thank Y[...]
~ma[...]
www.themaxmilesfoundation.[...]
mdmiksyeyahoo.com
323-627-4233

ALIVE! AND UNSTOPPABLE

How to Break Free from Dark Shadows

MARK DALE MILES

Foreword by Michael Bernard Beckwith

BALBOA.
PRESS

A DIVISION OF HAY HOUSE

Balboa Press books may be ordered through booksellers or by contacting:

Balboa Press
A Division of Hay House
1663 Liberty Drive
Bloomington, IN 47403
www.balboapress.com
1 (877) 407-4847

Because of the dynamic nature of the Internet, any web addresses or links contained in this book may have changed since publication and may no longer be valid. The views expressed in this work are solely those of the author and do not necessarily reflect the views of the publisher, and the publisher hereby disclaims any responsibility for them.

The author of this book does not dispense medical advice or prescribe the use of any technique as a form of treatment for physical, emotional, or medical problems without the advice of a physician, either directly or indirectly. The intent of the author is only to offer information of a general nature to help you in your quest for emotional and spiritual well-being. In the event you use any of the information in this book for yourself, which is your constitutional right, the author and the publisher assume no responsibility for your actions.

Scripture taken from the New King James Version®. Copyright © 1982 by Thomas Nelson. Used by permission. All rights reserved.

Any people depicted in stock imagery provided by Thinkstock are models, and such images are being used for illustrative purposes only.
Certain stock imagery © Thinkstock.

Print information available on the last page.

ISBN: 978-1-5043-7584-9 (sc)
ISBN: 978-1-5043-7586-3 (hc)
ISBN: 978-1-5043-7585-6 (e)

Library of Congress Control Number: 2017903063

Balboa Press rev. date: 04/20/2017

This book is dedicated to my nephew, Braxton Jecory Bell. You are strong and resilient and have everything that it takes to live an unstoppable life. And to all the people who have felt marginalized and disinherited, who fight against every obstacle to get back on track and to the truth of who you are: this book is for you. May it lead you to the next step on your inward and outward journey toward freedom.

ACKNOWLEDGMENTS

There are so many people who have helped me on this journey over the years. My life has been blessed beyond measure by the kindness of those around me. Their faith in me—in my ability to overcome and to thrive—has helped me more profoundly than I can express.

I would like to thank Mother Ruby Burruss, my spiritual mother who mentored me as a young man. She prayed for me, even after I had drifted from the church and fell into drugs. Through it all, she continued to see the best for me. She was a great intercessor and guide who showered me with unconditional love and helped me see what I was capable of accomplishing. I am grateful to my family, my brothers and sisters, aunts, uncles, cousins, nieces and nephews for being a part of my growing experience. I have learned many life lessons and those experiences have helped shape me and given me strength to endure and overcome any obstacle.

I like to thank Dean Sterling H. Hudson III from Morehouse College. Dean Hudson opened the Morehouse doors and allowed me to walk through. His courage and belief set the stage for me to change my life. I would like to thank Dr. John H. Stanfield II, Chairman of the Sociology department at Morehouse College. Dr. Stanfield took me under his wings and mentored me through Morehouse and beyond. He has championed me on my journey to sobriety and stayed committed to helping me to succeed with his constant support, assistance and prayer. I would like to thank Dr. Obie Clayton chairman of the Sociology Department at Morehouse College and Director of the Morehouse Research Institute and Mr. Travis Paton my supervisor for supporting me when times were tough. These men believed in me and allowed me the opportunity to work as a research assistant. Likewise, I am indebted to Annette Church Ingram, my Morehouse counselor, who prophesied on my life. She saw my future before I did and told me that I was going to be a minister. She supported me with her conviction and wisdom for many years.

I will forever be grateful to Mr. and Mrs. John "Sonny" and Mildred Hollins and their entire family for all that they have done for me especially when I was struggling with the loss of my mother and my addiction. My Morehouse brother James (Chris) Lee and his wife Ann Lee, my friends since high school, for always encouraging me to live the life that I wanted to live. For them, just being true to my own values regardless what other people think was more than enough. Robyn Maitland, who is both my life coach and my voice student, has always encouraged and inspired me to be my best self. Through her eyes I have learned to see myself as successful, fulfilled and living a life that I love. I especially thank her for always reminding me of the genius that's within me. William Strong my Morehouse brother and friend, who has supported me in all my endeavors from the academic to constructive literary criticism.

Also, I would like to thank Mrs. Woodie Persons, the founder and director of Gate City Heritage School in Atlanta where I worked as the music teacher for 12 years for allowing me to work in a field I love. I would like to thank the late Dr. Wendell P. Whalum Sr., former Chairman of the music department, Dr. Uzee Brown, my voice instructor and Dr. David Morrow, the director of the Morehouse College Glee Club for demonstrating and teaching me the art of excellence in music of which I shall take with me for the rest of my life.

I would like to thank Dr. Aaron Parker, pastor of Zion Hill Baptist Church in Atlanta and Morehouse professor, and Dr. Otis Moss III, pastor of Trinity United Church of Christ in Chicago. Both of these men encouraged me to write this book and tell my personal story in its pages, believing that my story could inspire others. I would like to thank Rev. Stephon Gillard who first saw and understood my call into the ministry. Rev. Gillard was an excellent pastor, mentor and friend during a significant spiritual transition in my life. I would like to thank Doris Ware for supporting me though seminary and while I was an associate minister at Pleasant Grove Missionary Baptist Church. Doris continues to be an excellent support and friend. Dr. Maisha Hazzard and Dr. Alexizena Hazzard have helped me develop the idea for this book, supporting and encouraging me throughout the writing process. Their insightful suggestions took this work to an even higher level than I could have ever imagined on my own. Dr. Eugene Herrington for introducing me to Landmark Education and that introduction continued on to coaching me through two theological seminary schools and for mentoring me all the way through graduation and beyond.

I would like to thank the entire Emory University family for pushing me past my limits and believing in my ability to obtain the Master of Divinity degree especially Dr. Teresa Fry Brown and Dr. Noel Leo Erskine. A special thanks to my cousin, Anthony D. Clinkscales for proofreading the final draft of the manuscript and providing important insights which enhanced the work, but even more for his work as a musician, minister and counselor.

To my editor, Kuwana Haulsey, who helped me bring the story of my life to these pages in such a beautiful and vivid way—thank you! Anita Rehker, Dr. Beckwith's wonderful editor who assisted us with the foreword, I am humbled by your encouragement and support.

Finally, I would like to thank Dr. Michael Bernard Beckwith and the entire Agape International Spiritual Center and New Thought community in Los Angeles CA. Studying with Dr. Beckwith opened me up to a richer understanding of God and stretched me in ways that allowed me to see God in places that I hadn't been able to see Him before. I thank Dean Lawrence E. Carter, Sr. from Morehouse for sending me to

Dr. Beckwith, where I was blessed to encounter teachings that changed my life.

The love and joy that you have all brought into my life has enriched it beyond measure. God bless you all!

TABLE OF CONTENTS

Acknowledgments vii

Foreword by Michael Bernard Beckwith xv

Preface 1

Chapter One
Deadbeats, Beggars and Bums: Breaking away
from limiting beliefs and the self-fulfilling
prophesies of the past 19

Chapter Two
Looking for Love and Found a Bullet: Making
choices that will change your life..................................... 37

Chapter Three
There are No Mistakes: Releasing mental
blocks and old beliefs to embrace new options 52

Chapter Four
What Must Be Done: Following through on the
spiritual truth about you.. 67

Chapter Five
Prophetic Voice vs. Pathetic Voice: Making the big
paradigm shift.. 83

Chapter Six
Fear is a Racket: Letting go of excuses and
negative coping skills... 98

Chapter Seven
Some Other to Win: Allowing your victories to
push you toward achieving your next big goal..............116

Chapter Eight
Not Here to Get, But Here to Let: Helping others
through giving 132

Chapter Nine
Drop the Material, See the Spiritual: "Walking
the bridge from reason to faith"....................................150

FOREWORD

The journey of Mark Dale Miles is one of the most courageous and triumphant testaments of trust in one's True Self that I've encountered in my 30 years of being in the ministry and counseling thousands of individuals. The trait connecting each step of his victory is his invincible commitment to walk the path of the spiritual warrior. The degree of challenge one faces in doing so is exceedingly high, so when saying that Mark is a qualified guide for all those who read this book, I do not do so lightly.

On the pages of *Alive and Unstoppable* unfolds the story of a harrowing childhood, one absent of positive role models, one filled with tormenting physical and verbal abuse from his father, with gang-involved youth, drug and alcohol addiction, racial profiling and prejudice, and a level of violence most of us encounter only through broadcast news or movies seen from the safety of our living room couch. Mark's inner and outer work with these life circumstances is a reminder of the inherent Wholeness that flows as naturally as blood through each and every one of us.

In a spirit of honest, raw self-disclosure, Mark holds back nothing of his own dark nights of the soul, proving that limitless possibilities and grace are withheld from no one who dares to redirect and reshape his or her life against seemingly impossible, heart shattering odds. When he tells us, "I knew that just because something was supposed to be impossible didn't mean that it would be impossible *for me*," we witness how his spirit-soul intuitively guides him to take actions that provide factual evidence to his self-empowering claim.

How do we stay committed to our intentions in spite of failing over and over again and the shame and discouragement that result? Mark's answer comes from his refusal to give up on himself, by accepting challenges as vehicles for removing obstacles to fulfilling his intentions. Having been recipients of abuse, how do we enable ourselves to forgive, to meet and engage with the world with a loving, compassionate heart? We can follow Mark's example of reprogramming our conscious and subconscious by taking ownership of our original innocence, intelligence, serenity, compassion, beauty, and being conscious co-creators of our life with our Creator Source.

Mark's elevating insights and undaunted heroic actions in each chapter of *Alive and Unstoppable* inspire trust in an assisting grace that is unconditionally available to us all. May his heartening message reach deep into your soul and awaken the spiritual warrior within.

Michael Bernard Beckwith
Agape International Spiritual Center
April 2017

PREFACE

"Go to bed!" The voice was clear, distinctive and would not be denied.

"Go to bed," it told me as I fell through the threshold of my front door, into the foyer, and face down on the floor. I struggled to get back to my feet, but somehow the entire left side of my body was paralyzed. Disoriented and confused, I focused my entire being on doing what the voice had just commanded me to do: go to bed.

I had no idea why I needed to lie down. I couldn't even remember how I had gotten home. My memory jumped from stopping at the bank on the way home for a little cash, to standing in my doorway with my key in the lock, to being inside my apartment laid out on the floor. I didn't even know whose voice had spoken to me. All I knew was that I needed to obey the command that I'd been given.

Go to bed!

It was only nine or ten at night. *Why would I be going to bed?* I wondered. But the voice in my head was adamant.

I dragged my body up off the floor and somehow managed to push the front door closed, engaging the security lock. When I tried to walk toward the bedroom I fell right back down. I pulled myself up again and when I did, I noticed a gray stain on the wall directly in front of me. It looked like little bits of splattered food. I later came to understand that the gummy substance was actually brain matter.

I'd been shot in the head at close range. But at the time, I had no idea what had happened to me. I didn't see any blood and couldn't recall being attacked. I just kept wondering why there was food on the wall and thinking that I needed to clean it off. But first—before I did anything else—I had to make it to the bedroom and lie down.

I staggered across the living room, collapsing straight through a glass coffee table. The glass shattered everywhere but amazingly I didn't cut myself. It took some time, but I was able to get back to my feet and stumble down the long hallway, past the bathroom and linen closet, toward the bedroom. I stripped off all my clothes and, just as the voice told me to do; I lay down on my back in my bed. It was summertime in Atlanta, hot and humid even at night. I'd left the air conditioning running when I left that morning so my apartment was very cold. The cold air didn't bother me, though, as I lay naked on the bed. I felt strangely comfortable and unafraid.

Again, I wondered what was happening and whose voice it was that kept speaking to me. The date was June 30, 2003, my mother's birthday. She had passed away a few years prior and I thought at first that perhaps it was her voice coming back to protect and watch over me. But that didn't make sense. *Dead people don't talk*, I reasoned.

The voice returned and this time it began to intone the 23rd Psalm, which reads: *The Lord is my shepherd, I shall not want. He makes me to lie down in green pastors; He leads me besides the still waters. He restores my soul; He leads me in the paths of righteousness for His namesake. Yea, though I walk through the valley of the shadow of death, I will fear no evil; for You are with me; Your rod and Your staff they comfort me. You prepare a table before me in the presence of my enemies; You anoint my head with oil; my cup runs over. Surely goodness and mercy shall follow me all the days of my life; And I will dwell in the house of the Lord Forever.* (NKJV)

The psalm told me that I should not fear for the Lord was with me. I believed it and was not afraid. That's how I came to realize that the voice in my head was the voice of God, protecting and keeping me. As I lay on my back, I felt this powerful presence wash over me. It was assured and comforting, commanding and yet overflowing with the energy of abiding, unconditional love.

For many hours, my attention drifted back and forth between the voice in my mind and the voices on the television, which had been on the entire time. I listened to newscasters discuss the happenings of the day. Kobe Bryant had been caught cheating. Barry White passed away. Lester Maddox the 75th governor of Georgia and Maynard Jackson the 54th and the 56th mayor of Atlanta had both recently passed away.

Then, cutting through all the background noise, the voice spoke again. It told me that my life had been going in a direction that would keep me from doing what I had been called to do, what I had actually prayed for. I realized that I had, in fact, prayed for an intervention in my life just days before.

I'd been working as a counselor for the Summer Institute at my alma mater, Morehouse College. It was a big project where we brought in young men from all over the country to participate in our extensive summer curriculum. Many of these boys were poor, inner city kids who had lived through horrible traumas such as watching mothers and sisters being raped in front of them and being unable to protect them. Some of the boys had even been sexually assaulted themselves. They were dealing with the absence of father figures, drugs running rampant through their homes and communities, high incarceration levels and more. It was incredible to me that these young men would have to face these kinds of hardships.

The experience moved me to want to do better, to know more in order to really help them in ways that I felt they deserved. I'd walked across campus thinking about what more I could do and ended up standing in front of the gravesite of renowned Morehouse president, Dr. Benjamin E. Mays. I knelt down at his grave and prayed for guidance. I prayed for

God to pull me up to the next level of understanding so that I might be able to help these young men change their lives, rather than just feel sorry for them or offer superficial aid. I needed more skills in order to really be effective. From what I learned in my childhood church, we call the type of prayer that I prayed that day an *effectual fervent prayer*. I prayed with all my might that God would intervene in my life, as well as in the lives of these young men. I also got a deeper realization of a powerful quote I once read stating *when God is all we got, God is all we need*. In that moment I realized that only prayer could help me in my time of need. I prayed this prayer on June 28, 2003.

Two days later teenaged boys put a bullet in my head. Of course, I didn't realize that my answered prayer could come in such a form. But that's what happened. And it was the beginning of a journey that changed every aspect of my life forever.

For the next three days, I laid in that bed unable to move. Then, on the third day, I heard a booming noise at the front of the house. Someone was trying to break down my front door. They kicked at the door repeatedly, each noise louder than the last. But they couldn't get in because the security lock was engaged.

Finally I'm being rescued! I thought. But after a few minutes the noise stopped. I listened thinking that any minute I would hear the voice of policemen or EMT workers calling out to see if I was okay. Nothing happened. Then I heard the sound of my patio door quietly sliding open. That's when I realized that the perpetrators were back. The people who had hurt me (I still wasn't quite sure what had been done to me, but I knew that I had been hurt) had returned to finish what they'd started.

Suddenly a group of seven or eight young black men walked into my bedroom. They were teenagers, unmasked and unconcerned about being caught because they must have believed that I was dead. They walked in right past me and began rifling through my closets and dresser drawers. At that point, I raised my head to see what they were doing. The boys jumped back in fear.

Seeing that I wasn't dead, one of them grabbed a sock from my drawer and tried to wrap it around the lower part of his face, as though that would keep me from recognizing him later.

"Why are you in my apartment?" I asked.

Slowly they moved toward me. Once they figured out that I couldn't move, they went back to what they'd been doing, rifling through all of my things and taking what they wanted. One of them stepped boldly toward me. The boy, who looked like he was no more than 14-years-old, picked up a pillow off the floor.

He looked me straight in the face and said, "I'm going to smother you."

"Young man, put that pillow down!" I ordered. "Get out of here!" The strength of my voice shocked us all.

But he continued to move closer. As he reached over me with the pillow another boy, who looked to be about 15 or 16-years-old, stepped between us and stopped him.

"Man, let's go," he said. "Don't kill him. Let's go."

I'd been called to work with young men like these. I've given everything to try to help them get beyond the circumstances of their lives. And yet here I was at the mercy of these boys, who could've easily been my students.

One of them leaned over me and asked if I wanted some water. This boy looked like he was about seventeen. He walked out of the bedroom toward the kitchen. A moment later he returned with a gallon of water in one hand and a bottle of Bayer aspirin in the other. But I was disoriented and paranoid by this time. As he held the bottle of water out to me I became convinced that the boy and his friends were trying to poison me.

"Get that away from me!" I said. "I don't want that." I refused the water even though I was literally dying of dehydration. I couldn't understand why the boy was trying to give me an aspirin when I didn't even have a headache. Nothing made any sense.

Though I'd refused the water, I knew I needed something to drink. There was a bottle of water on my dresser that I'd been looking at for the last three days. It was only a twelve-ounce bottle, and half full at that, but I said to the boy, "if you can get me that water right there I'll drink it."

The boy held the bottle up to my mouth and I drained every last drop. As I looked around at their faces and realized that I knew one of them from the complex. They called him Shorty. He was the oldest, probably about 21-years-old at the time. I had even talked to him once or twice outside the community pool. Why would they have decided to rob me? I had never had any trouble with Shorty or any of these boys. Why would they target me in such a violent way? Was it some sort of gang initiation? A random home invasion?

A few minutes later the boys left. The apartment was quiet until the following evening, when more men came. These men were older. They barely looked at me as they grabbed whatever they could carry and carted it away. My apartment was like an open secret for the criminals in the neighborhood. On the fifth evening an older man came in alone. He appeared to be in his 40's, with dark skin and blood shot eyes. As he searched through my closet he told me he was with the police and that he would be getting help out to me very soon.

But he looked so cruel and terrifying that I closed my eyes and turned my head away from him. I became painfully aware of being paralyzed and naked on my bed, drenched in sweat and urine, completely vulnerable. I didn't care about the things that he took. I just prayed that he wouldn't harm me. He didn't. He just walked out with the last of my valuables.

On the sixth day and night nobody arrived at my apartment. There wasn't anything left to steal. I began to wonder if I was going to die there alone. Then, on the seventh afternoon, I heard someone open the front door and walk back toward the bedroom. It was my friend Mike Mike.

Mike Mike was a young man I knew from the community that I'd been trying to build a friendship with. We'd hang out and I would drive him around to different places in my car. He was 27-years-old at the time, a full ten years younger than me. Back then I tended to befriend people who were significantly younger than me because, deep inside, I didn't feel like I was on the same level as my peers. Hanging out with younger people gave me a sense of feeling respected and in control. Mike Mike was slim with long braided hair, a handsome face and a very polite, respectful demeanor. I'd even gotten to know his family. In my mind, Mike Mike was a good person and a loyal friend. I was happy to see him standing in my bedroom doorway.

Mike Mike looked down at me lying on the bed and said, "I don't want you to die."

Then he picked me up and dragged me out of the bed toward the bathroom. As he lifted me, the skin from my back and my buttocks and the back of my legs peeled off my body. There had been a plastic mattress protector under my sheet and over the course of the week, when I had urinated on myself, the liquid stayed trapped around my body, eventually eating away my skin. My kidneys had already begun to shut down.

Mike Mike dragged me into the tub and left me there, promising that he would be back shortly. He did return a few minutes later with another friend. He pulled me up out of the tub and asked which way I wanted to go—back to the bedroom or into the living room. I was suddenly aware of the stench of urine that made the bedroom unbearable. I told Mike Mike to take me to the living room and sit me down on the sofa. He brought some underwear from the bedroom and pulled it up over my naked body. Then he handed me my class ring from college and my car keys.

Why would Mike Mike have my things? I wondered. I noticed that he was also wearing a white polo shirt of mine as well. That's when I began to wonder if Mike Mike had been the one who set me up. I wondered if Mike Mike was the reason that those boys had targeted me in the first place.

I looked up at Mike Mike's friend and asked him to please call 911. The man said, "I'm not going to call 911. I'm not getting involved in this." So I told Mike Mike to call, "I need you to dial 911." Mike Mike turned to his friend and said, "Hey man, call 911." The man still refused. "I'm not calling," he said adamantly. So Mike Mike jerked the phone from the man's hand and said, "I'll do it myself." He told the dispatcher that there was an injured man who needed immediate assistance at my address. Then he and his friend left before the authorities could arrive.

The police made it to my house before the ambulance. The officers were asking me all kinds of questions that I couldn't answer, trying to piece together what had happened. But nothing I said added up. They wanted to know why there was no forced entry or other signs pointing to how the robbers got inside. I couldn't explain.

Luckily, the paramedics arrived a few minutes later, placed me on a stretcher and rolled me into the back of the ambulance. On July 7th, at around 4:00 in the afternoon, I finally arrived at Emory Medical Center. I lay there on the stretcher in the emergency ward until around 9:00 in the evening waiting for my turn to be examined. The doctors couldn't determine what was wrong with me or why I was experiencing pain in my neck and spine. One of the doctors put his hand on my forehead and I yelled, "Ouch!" He looked closer and found a wound at the top of my forehead near the hairline that had been clotted over with blood. This made him very suspicious and he insisted that an MRI be done.

Around 10:00 that evening, a group of about six or seven doctors, followed by a detective and two police officers, entered my room. The doctor said, "Mr. Miles, do you know that you've been shot?"

"Where have I been shot?" I asked.

He replied, "You've been shot in the head."

I was stunned. But it did make sense, considering the paralysis and the memory loss. *Well*, I thought to myself. *I can still think. I'm still me. My mind is still intact.*

"So," I asked slowly, "what does that mean?"

The doctor explained, "Well, the damage has been done. The bullet is in fragments. Part of it stayed in the front of your head and part of it migrated all the way to the back of your skull, down near your neck. That must be why you're experiencing neck and back pain. But it can't be removed. So, how you heal from this point forward depends on you—on your commitment to rehabilitate yourself. It will depend on your dedication to your speech therapy, occupational therapy and physical therapy.

"You know," he continued, "it was very lucky for you that you were able to lay down on your back like that."

"Why?" I asked.

"In that position the blood was able to clot very quickly. You had very little blood loss at all. If you hadn't lain down, the wound would have stayed open and you would have bled to death. You are a miracle, Mr. Miles."

The doctor's words weren't surprising. I knew that I had been given the call for a reason—and with a purpose.

Later on, after I had rested a little, the police came back and informed me that they had found marijuana in my apartment.

"That explains the motive for robbery," one of the officers told me. "That's what they were looking for."

Seven people were ultimately taken in for questioning in relation to the shooting and the robbery. They were found with my belongings stuffed into a duffel bag. But, to the best of my knowledge, no one was ever convicted. Because of my memory loss I wasn't able to give police a reliable statement about what had led up to my being shot or identify any of the boys who robbed me, other than the young man Shorty. And I wouldn't sign off on the statement written up by police because I wasn't certain it was accurate.

Instead, I focused all of my thoughts and energy on rehabilitating myself. During the rehab process, I began to learn what it meant to truly be unstoppable. In the beginning, the only parts on the left side of my body that I could move were my fingertips. I'd watch my fingertips intently and tell myself, *if you can move your fingertips, then you can move the rest of your hand.*

Through extensive therapy I ultimately regained the use of my hand and the left side of my body. I re-learned how to write and how to read by reading children's books like The Story of Noah. I had to re-learn basic life skills like how to dress myself and cook and drive. My therapist and I used children's matching games to strengthen my damaged memory. But no matter how difficult things became I refused to give up. One day my occupational therapist looked at me in disbelief and she asked, "How are you doing all of this?"

Given the nature of my injuries I wasn't supposed to be able to accomplish even simple tasks. But I'd already decided that I was going to defy all of their expectations. I had just graduated from Morehouse College after 14 years of hard struggle, persevering through family tragedies and poverty and substance abuse relapses to finally earn my degree. No one was going to tell me that I could no longer think, that I could no longer work that I wouldn't be able to use the things that I'd learned to make my life better and to improve the lives of others. It was simply not going to happen, no matter what the experts said. I was determined to get my life back.

One of my therapists, Dr. Milton Young, was inspired by my progress and he believed in me. He always encouraged me to go further. With his support, I eventually decided that I was going to apply for a Masters degree. I figured that a rigorous Masters program at a world-renowned university could be a new form of cognitive therapy. It would help me strengthen my ability to think and solve problems and engage in advanced forms of communication again.

Not only did I graduate from a Masters program at Webster University, I ultimately received a second Masters degree in theology from Candler School of Theology at Emory University. This was supposed to be impossible for someone with permanent learning disabilities, but I refused to be stopped by conventional thinking. I knew that just because something was supposed to be impossible didn't mean that it would be impossible *for me*.

Though my experience was extreme, everyone comes to these kinds of crossroads in life. And everyone has the ability to become unstoppable. In my case, I had to realize that long-suffering was a necessary part of my process. Rather than seeking to rush through the intensely difficult areas of my life, I had to lean in and realize that in my toughest moments my character was being built. I became present to the seriousness of the call on my life. Before that time, I'd been in spiritual limbo. I had made progress but it was very, very slow. I recognize now that God had been trying to deal with me for a very long time about negative behaviors and negative people that I'd allowed into my life. But I hadn't been ready or willing to release them.

It's common for people to hold on to the things that are dragging them down. I couldn't let go of the negative influences in my life until they caused me to have a bullet lodged in my brain. That bullet will be there for the rest of my life, a reminder of what happens when I refuse to heed my call to move forward.

Over time, God was able to show me the part that I played in the situation that almost caused me to lose my life. I came to understand that the trauma I experienced was a necessary part of my spiritual evolution; God used that experience to pull me out of an ordinary life into an extraordinary life. The Spirit of God was seeking to elevate me to a secret place, a place where He dwells and where I would dwell with Him. The boy who shot me meant to kill me, but God used him instead to get my attention so that He could redirect my life.

That young boy actually did me a favor because my old path wouldn't have allowed God to work through me in the way that I had wanted and had prayed for and that was possible for me.

Go lie down was the initial call that God gave me, in the same way that Moses' initial call was *take off your shoes*. The initial call is what puts us on the path toward finding and fulfilling our purpose on the planet. When a person gets a call it means that there's another way of living, a job or an assignment that must be fulfilled, which only that person can do.

Everyone has been called to do something. However, so often people miss the call on their lives because they don't believe that they're here for any meaningful or worthwhile purpose. Sometimes they miss the call because they're distracted by the world, by materialism or social norms. They may become sidetracked as their families grow and their external responsibilities increase. Sometimes old habits, fears and insecurities become distractions that keep us small and stuck, unable to move into the expansive new places that God has prepared. Sometimes there is no distraction. There's just an unwillingness to accept the responsibilities that come along with these monumental changes.

But once you say yes, a shift starts to take place. It becomes possible to grasp the meaning of your call, to contextualize it in a way that can bring clarity to the assignment. This process may require you to give up behaviors or views that you hold dear. Sometimes you have to change how you see yourself.

Oftentimes, we don't feel like we're important enough or good enough or smart enough to really affect change in the world. We can feel as though we aren't prepared enough to answer the call that we've been given. We start negotiating with ourselves, coming up with all the reasons why we're not capable or willing to answer the call. This is where and how we get stopped in our lives.

We become unstoppable when we say *yes*, when we move toward what we're being asked to do regardless of what circumstances look like or what the naysayers may predict. The willingness to move toward the call, even if we don't know where we're going or how we're going to get there, is all that we need to become unstoppable.

No matter what comes up in life, no matter what situations you've faced, no matter what crime you may have committed, what place you may have come from or what addiction you may have wrestled with, you get to say how your life turns out. You get to say whether you go to the next level or whether you're stopped by circumstance.

There's no condition or situation that can determine your destiny. As William Earnest Henley wrote, "I am the master of my fate; I am the captain of my soul. I thank whatever gods may be for my unconquerable soul". It is very important to understand that in order to have your destiny realized you also need the right tools to do the job that you've been called to do.

That is the purpose of this book: to give you the tools to become unstoppable in your own life. This book will help teach you how to maintain your focus and how to build a life that you love. It will help you to gain clarity and insight into your purpose for being here on the planet at this time. You don't have to believe any of the negative things that people have said about you or even the things that you said about yourself. You get to choose again and again and again who you are and which direction your life is going to go. This book is about becoming conscious to that process and choosing, on a daily basis, to keep moving in the direction of greatness.

CHAPTER ONE

Deadbeats, Beggars and Bums:
Breaking away from limiting beliefs and
the self-fulfilling prophesies of the past

My maternal grandparents had a total of 14 children but sadly two died shortly after birth. My mother was the oldest daughter and she had seven children of her own. Ours was a huge, close-knit family and we all depended heavily on our grandparents for support. All of the children and grandchildren would visit regularly and congregate at our grandparent's house for all of the different holidays and get-togethers and had a goodtime singing, eating and fellowshipping. But we also showed up when we didn't have anywhere else to stay. At one point, my family had been burned out of our home. So we showed up at my grandparent's door looking to be taken in. Several of the other children and grandchildren also took turns going back home when life wasn't working out for them the way they had hoped. Even my grandfather's mother-in-law lived with them for a time.

My grandfather was a hard-working man who bought a large, comfortable home in the white section of our town in Anderson, South Carolina. Then he built more rooms onto his house so the house had about five or six bedrooms altogether. He was proud that there was plenty of room for the family, but at the same time it angered him to see his children and grandchildren so unstable.

My grandfather worked at the local elementary and middle school as the groundskeeper and janitor. He was responsible for doing things like lighting the wood-burning stove to keep them warm during the winter. He also worked at the town's mill. On top of that, he was the head deacon in the church and was responsible for maintaining and cleaning that building, too. My maternal grandmother took care of the 12 children. But at times she labored outside of the home as a domestic.

Both of my grandparents valued hard work and discipline. My grandfather expected his children to contribute their incomes to his household once they were grown and working, for as long as they lived with him. They were raising a huge family in the years following the depression. Times were hard and everyone was expected to pitch in.

Eventually, when the children got old enough to think about getting married and starting families of their own, they rebelled. They wanted to keep their money for themselves so they could get out and make their own way in life. My grandfather became upset and bitter that his children refused to contribute their incomes even though they were living under his roof. And the ones who had left home already were constantly returning, expecting him and my grandmother to provide stability.

With twelve children and their families relying on him my grandfather changed. He'd lash out at whoever was around; telling anyone who would listen that his family was always begging and borrowing from him. We were so needy and useless. Even though he'd set the example of being a hard worker who was frugal with his money, he didn't seem to be able to pass those values along to the majority of his children.

Nothing could stop my grandfather from getting up and going out to work. As he grew older, he developed a physical disability that made walking painful. He eventually began to walk with a limp. Completing his job duties became increasingly difficult due to his physical limitations. But when he would call the children to come help him, quite often no one showed up except for one or two of the girls helping out with paying the bills and bringing the groceries as they got older. As far as he was concerned everyone expected help when they needed it but they weren't willing to offer help in return.

As a child, I remember hearing my grandfather constantly complaining. "They're all deadbeats, beggars and bums," he would grumble.

I do believe that my grandfather really loved us—particularly me because he allowed me to live in his basement when I returned home from college and needed to get away from my father just before a very bad addiction to drugs. But he couldn't get past his belief that we were all deadbeats, beggars and bums and would never amount to anything else. No matter what I did, it was seldom good enough. I loved to sing and was learning to play the piano and I was becoming good at it. But when I would go practice more often than not my grandfather would yell, "Stop that noise! Get off that piano!" He couldn't hear much good from me (or any of us) that countered his deeply held belief.

But constantly drawing a person's attention to his or her perceived shortcomings doesn't help that person to actually change for the better. Most of my grandfather's children and grandchildren continued to demonstrate the traits that he found so repulsive. After a while I stopped feeling anything about him and his tirades. I even stopped feeling an emotional connection to myself. I had no self-esteem, low or high. I became numb.

People can easily become affected by the words and beliefs of those around them, especially authority figures like parents and grandparents and teachers. The Bible says in Proverbs 22:6, "Train up a child in the way that he should go and when he is old he will not depart from it." (NKJV) But this also works in reverse. When you train up a child by steeping him or her in negativity, it's very difficult for the child to break through the limiting beliefs that have been instilled in the subconscious mind. In my family we were taught many lessons of inferiority, which we acted out as adults.

I first began to think about the differences between positive and negative reinforcement when I noticed an interesting trend happening with some of the families who married into our family. When children were born, sometimes the in-laws would become the driving force in raising and teaching the grandchildren instead of people from our side of the family. Over the years, those children grew up to do wonderful things with their lives. They were instilled with an entirely different set of core beliefs and self-talk. In contrast, the majority of people from my mother's side of the family didn't show any high levels of motivation or ambition. My family members were as bright, personable, talented and able to achieve as anyone else. So what happened?

A person's core belief system is a powerful predictor of performance levels and the ability to succeed. In other words, you get what you believe you deserve in life—not what you actually want or are capable of having. If someone set low expectations for you in the past, you will live out those expectations to the extent that you believed the person who set them. Sometimes we can even start to believe that our station in life is "God's will," or something that is completely outside of our control. Nothing could be further from the truth. But we must embrace our innate power to transform our lives into exactly what we wish for them to become.

One way to begin this transformation is by becoming aware of your gifts and talents and began developing them. For example, I loved to sing. So I joined singing groups, school choirs, church choirs and the 4-H club. I went anywhere that people wanted to hear me sing. As challenging as it was for me at first, I put myself out there. I got involved. One of the singing groups I remember singing with as a child was started up by my grandfather called The Baby Brothers course of which I was a founding member. Singing with that group was one of the rare times I was able to get acceptance and shown unconditional love from my grandfather. He was extremely proud of the young men he requited in the group and he demonstrated it by having us practice in his home once or twice a week and by providing snacks and drinks afterwards. More than 35 years later The Baby Brothers course is still intact and continues singing every Sunday night at my home church back in South Carolina.

Getting involved can be very difficult to do, especially if your belief in yourself as someone talented and good has been compromised. But try. The response that you receive when you earnestly offer your gifts to the world will change your life.

As you commit to sharing your gifts and trying new things, look for a mentor whose example can help you move in the direction that you wish to go. Ever since I was a young man, I sought out mentors to help guide me. Their presence in my life made all the difference. When my own family was full of stress, strife and negativity, these people showed me that I could move beyond my circumstances. One of my earliest mentors was the Bishop's wife at my childhood church; she gave me encouragement and spiritual teachings that help me to begin believing in myself. No one had ever done that for me before. She sowed seeds of wisdom and compassion in my heart that continue to bear fruit, even to this day.

Another very powerful technique for dismantling a limiting belief system is the art of journaling. You can explore in depth the things that may be blocking you and keeping you stuck. You can get clarity on where you want to go in life. Many times people who have low self-esteem, low expectations or feelings of unworthiness become just like I was: emotionally numb or even depressed. From that state of mind, it's difficult to figure out what one really wants out of life or which direction is the best. If this is the case, journaling can open the door to identifying your true feelings and desires.

For me, I was so far removed from my own feelings and needs that there was another step I had to take before I was ready to even begin journaling. I had to start by looking for inspiration outside of myself. I began to make friends with people who were moving in a positive direction. I actively sought out people who had embraced uplifting beliefs and worldviews. They set lofty goals for themselves and then did the work to achieve those goals. I watched them move through the world, learning what I could as their presence and demeanor shifted my own ability to see myself.

I would go and spend the night at friends' houses and watch carefully how their families engaged with each other; I noted all the ways that they encouraged and rewarded and even corrected one another. The healthiest environments were the ones where people communicated with love, acceptance and positive expectation rather than shaming or putdowns. The parents offered praise and appreciation for their children when they did well in school. They took advantage of opportunities to reaffirm their support in other areas of their children's lives as well.

For the first time, I realized how destructive my "normal" environment had been. As I watched my friends and their families, I began to *feel* how I wanted my life to look. It was no longer just an intellectual idea or a fleeting hope. I surrounded myself with positive energy until I was able to recognize and embrace the same flow of energy within me. Never lose sight of the fact that it can happen for you, too. You may not get this kind of connection from your family of origin, but there are other places and other ways of having these desires fulfilled.

But when you're living a negative, self-fulfilling prophecy based on someone else's idea of who you are there isn't much room for you to fulfill your deepest needs. Yet, we can still identify these needs by becoming present to the internal void that indicates what has been missing. Most people loathe confronting those empty spaces within, the fears and doubts that tell us what's wrong. But we must face our fears in order to embrace the insights on the other side of the void. Unfortunately, it can be much easier to point out what we don't want, rather than being able to explain what it is that we *do* want in life. At least in the beginning. But once you identify those driving needs, you can insert yourself into situations and circumstances where those needs have a chance of being fulfilled.

I had an undeniable need to honor my own greatness and my innate talents through my passion for singing. I fulfilled that desire by singing wherever I could. I gave my gift to others in order to feed my own burgeoning sense of self-worth. And even though my father and grandfather constantly discouraged me from performing, eventually my persistence was rewarded outside of my family.

As a 14-year-old boy, I was asked to sing happy birthday for President Ronald Reagan when he visited South Carolina that year. Reagan then invited me to Washington, DC to attend his inauguration. When that happened, my family was proud. But there was a whole internal process of self-revelation that was occurring, which allowed me to be brave enough to expose my most vulnerable areas. When I sang, I felt that I was fulfilling my life's purpose; I knew that I had something to bring to the table. I had worth and value. For the first time, I questioned whether the things that I'd always been told about myself were even true. Maybe I was capable of more than I'd ever dreamed.

The limiting beliefs that I'd been taught had been passed from my grandfather to his children, to his grandchildren, and later, to his great-grandchildren. His misdirected thoughts and energy become part of the family's emotional legacy. My father also created the atmosphere that allowed that emotional legacy to flourish. He used to tell me to my face that I was a mistake. He would regularly give me emotional, verbal and very severe physical beatings.

My father often said things like, "The more I try to teach him the dumber he gets." He never came to a baseball game or to hear me sing unless by the persuasion of my mother at occasional Sunday evening church programs. The only time he took part in any musical activity was the all-expenses-paid trip to Washington, DC that the family received for Reagan's inauguration. Aside from that, my father agreed with my grandfather's assessment that I couldn't do anything right.

My father was obviously a man in tremendous pain. I never knew what had caused that pain. I just knew that he tried to drink it away. There were things that he needed to deal with and never knew how to address. So his deep and painful self-worth issues were passed down to me. That was his legacy. In the same way that some families pass down money, heirlooms or family wisdom, my father unconsciously passed down his despair. Without realizing it, I took his issues on as my own. As hurtful as this was, I now realize that this kind of transference is an extremely common experience.

As we walk our path toward freedom, one of the key things that we must do is distinguish which thoughts and feelings are truly our own versus what we've inherited from our past, our families and our communities. As children we believe what we're told because that's what children do. By the time we grow into adulthood we tend not to question our deeply held beliefs, even if they don't serve our growth and happiness. Becoming conscious of these thoughts, trends and patterns can unravel the threads that have bound the generations together. Then we get to choose to keep what is life affirming while discarding those threads and beliefs that have held us in fear, doubt and feelings of worthlessness.

This is a difficult process. But part of our healing comes from knowing that we get to decide who we want to be now, in the present. We can deflect negativity by practicing positive self-talk and saying something like, "These negative beliefs are not who I am. I may have done some unhealthy things in the past but who I am now is a person of positivity and power and grace." If you can determine the source of any negative self-concepts that you have, that's great. It makes it that much easier to release them. But if you can't identify the source you can still dissolve them from your mental, emotional and energetic body.

One of the strategies that I used when I was trying to get away from the pervasive negativity surrounding me was to literally escape, to steal away from the energy so that I could re-create myself. It's very difficult to re-create yourself if you continue to be surrounded by the influences that helped produce a false sense of self in the first place. So take a trip. Apply to school in another state. Start a new career that you love. Learn some new skills. This process requires making a conscious decision about who we want to be, as well as feeling into the truth of who we really are—the talents, gifts and abilities that we were born to deliver. Allow your talents to manifest and your inner voice to direct your path.

Every new or latent talent that you discover will need to be cultivated. So you must not be afraid to invest in yourself. If you've lived with false beliefs or succumb to thoughts of unworthiness, it can seem selfish and counterproductive to start investing in your own joy and curiosity. But you must become present and committed to the things that matter to you.

When I decided that I wanted to go to college, I was already in my senior year of high school. The kids around me laughed and told me that I would never get into a good college like Morehouse, which is where I decided that I wanted to go. I had a 1.6 GPA at that time. But I decided to invest in myself. So I repeated my senior year of high school and graduated with a 3.4 GPA. Though I still wasn't able to get into Morehouse straight away, I was able to get into a good college, which positioned me to continue on with my dream.

The most important thing about this process was that I stopped believing the lie that I couldn't learn. For my entire life up until that point, I didn't realize that I'd been living a lie. I'd completely believed what my father, peers and other teachers had told me: that there was something wrong with me. When I got brave enough to challenge that reality, I realized that it was baseless. Those ideas were other people's beliefs acting as truth in my life.

When I did the work required to change my attitude and my outcomes, the entire world opened up. Taking the appropriate action steps is critical to our ability to make lasting changes. It seems as though this piece should be self-explanatory. Unfortunately, sometimes we feel called to do something or we're really passionate about changing our lives, but we don't actually take the actions necessary to make a difference. The possibilities remain as mere wishes in our minds. They never become actualized through the hard work of change.

Growing up I have been taught faith without works is dead. And there is always more to do. If you want a job sometimes it may not be enough to just fill out an application. You may have to show up and ask for an appointment to speak to the hiring manager. You may have to follow up with phone calls until you get the result that you want. Most people are comfortable with the idea of putting forth regular action to get what they want. But what we're talking about here is unstoppable action.

Unstoppable action is when you're told no but you still won't relent. You push past the no. If you're not accepted to the college of your choice, raise the standard of your work and then apply again. If you're told no, re-apply again. Then go down for an interview. Then write letters. Then ask other people to write letters on your behalf. Do whatever it takes to turn that no into a yes.

Unstoppable action requires being unreasonable in some ways. And some people will try to stop you. Sometimes it's nothing personal against you, but they're just doing what they think they need to do. Sometimes it is personal. Someone may think you've gotten too self-important or raised your expectations too high. But remember that you are the lens through which they are seeing themselves as well. So sometimes your growth can make people uncomfortable when they aren't ready or willing to grow themselves. That is none of your concern.

Put those people firmly out of your mind and concentrate on creating positive self-fulfilling prophecies. Speak your word out into the universe. Claim what you want and what you envision happening for you and how you're intending your life to unfold. You can speak your word into existence. It's your world, your life, your journey. You get to say how you want to experience life every step of the way. If you don't practice an intentional and purposeful way of living, you'll be like everyone else who's at the mercy of circumstance. Say, declare, decree and expect what you want to unfold in your life.

The act of declaring is both a principle and a tool for self-revelation. Declare and stand firm for what you believe until it happens. Sometimes it happens quickly and sometimes it happens very, very slowly. But it will happen as you continue to declare it.

While you're going along this path take the time to encourage others. So many people around us are suffering and being stopped by what they believe to be immovable mountains. Speak the truth to those people. Not only will you help them fulfill their dreams, but it's also a wonderful way to see your goals fulfilled even faster than you ever dreamed possible because of the positive energy that you're putting forth into the world. We all need someone to help us. Be that person who helps others. This also changes your mental construct for how you see yourself. Instead of seeing yourself as unworthy or a deadbeat (as my grandfather used to say) you can see yourself as someone who has something powerful and necessary to give. In this way you become abundantly clear that your life has meaning. Once you see how people listen to you and how you have risen out of the pull of those limiting beliefs, you'll see how far your reach really extends.

This is a paradigm shift that starts within. We're talking about shifting our entire belief systems around who we are and what we can achieve. What you thought you knew about yourself before you began this work will be completely different than what you discover as you move through the process. As you continue to live out these discoveries, and take chances and reevaluate everything you thought you knew, that's when the paradigm shifts. As you look back you'll be encouraged to continue further down this road, building on all your new discoveries.

Reflections

I related to...

CHAPTER TWO

Looking for Love and Found a Bullet:
Making choices that will change your life

Being shot in the head was an introductory call that changed the direction of my life forever. It took tremendous inner work for me to be able to see past the experience of being victimized in a brutal home invasion to the spiritual truth of the situation. In the process, I came to understand that part of my experience was due to my own choices.

There were certain people that I knew were negative influences, yet I chose to keep them around. I was seeking companionship and acceptance from individuals who didn't actually care about me. In other words, I was looking for love and found a bullet instead. Acknowledging the part that I played in creating my own painful circumstances was the first critical step toward change.

In order to grow spiritually or emotionally we must own our choices and the outcomes of those choices. Only then are we able to do something different, to create the kinds of internal changes that enable us to move forward. So often it's not until we experience severe consequences that we really look at how our decisions impact the circumstances of our lives. Once we're able to own our part in the outcomes that we experience, we can release the belief that we are somehow victims in life. We recognize our roles as active participants instead, which is much more powerful.

Of course, there's a big difference between recognizing that we play a part in the creation of our circumstances and giving in to self-blame around those circumstances. Sometimes people make the mistake of blaming themselves for everything that goes wrong, believing that they are somehow bad or responsible for negative events. But self-blame is always counterproductive. It's another way that victimhood shows up, which is completely different than taking responsibility for our own behaviors.

Shaming or beating ourselves up isn't the answer. Instead, we must honestly take stock of the areas in which we may need to grow and expand so that we can make healthier choices. For me, I had to reconcile with a deep-rooted need to feel needed. There was a void inside me that I desperately wanted to fill. But the people I chose to surround myself with couldn't possibly have filled the void, because they really didn't know why they were there. Unfortunately, I didn't know how to identify or communicate my real needs.

When we make choices that aren't in our best interest and that don't serve the greater good, we're usually trying to fill a deep-seated spiritual need. But nothing of this world can fulfill the longing to reconnect with our spiritual source. Yet we continue to look for connection and validation from other people or things. Moreover, without a measure of spiritual awareness we tend to seek things that have the power to pull us off our path. Certain choices may even cost us our lives—which is what nearly happened to me.

I was a single male who wanted companionship, whether from a man or from a woman. I sought sex, attention and approval in relationships that turned out to be dead-ends. For a time I believed that my friend Mike Mike (the man who ultimately betrayed me by setting up the robbery) could provide me with the support I craved. But shortly before I was robbed, I'd had a huge fight with Mike Mike about drugs, sex and money.

I'd been trying to develop a real relationship with him, but on the down low. Mike Mike, however, had been using me. He made all kinds of demands on me. He'd insisted that I provide him with marijuana, which was the price he wanted me to pay to continue to have him in my life. We fought because I discovered that Mike Mike had been seeing other people and had contracted an STD. The huge blowout that followed threatened to end our relationship. Mike Mike realized that he wasn't going to get what he wanted from me and he left. I took the drugs that I had scored for him and hid them away, thinking that was the end of the situation. A few days later I was shot and left for dead.

Back in those days I didn't see the conflict in spending time, money and energy on someone who only wanted to use me. I could've blamed Mike Mike for his actions and everything that resulted from them. But I came to understand that I'd been incapable of looking past the need for sex and companionship, which I confused with real caring and love. My outlook was completely distorted. I was in an identity crisis, shifting from the hurt, loss and rejection of the girlfriends in my life and trying to find what I was missing in men.

Because of my demeanor people often asserted that I was gay. Girlfriends, male friends and people in my community had insisted that I was gay so many times that I began to question myself. I realized that I hadn't been able to keep a strong, healthy heterosexual relationship together and began to wonder if other people knew me better than I knew myself. The woman that I had been the most in love with had never been willing to have an intimate relationship with me. And yet she had become pregnant by another man that she met and dated behind my back. This destroyed my confidence. Another girlfriend told me that she couldn't date me because her pastor had told her that I wasn't holy enough. This pattern had played out again and again from the beginning of my dating life. I could recall the mother of one girlfriend informing me that her daughter was too young to date and would no longer be able to see me. I was devastated.

For years, I carried feelings of insecurity and inadequacy into my relationships. I didn't know who I was or what I truly wanted. It was during this time that I also became heavily involved in drugs. So there was an added component that the women I met while I was abusing drugs weren't the kind of women that I felt safe or comfortable having a relationship with. On the other hand, I somehow found the men surrounding me more acceptable, even though those relationships were all about short-term companionship. The types of men that I pursued in those days were other men on the down low. These men didn't value me or what I brought to the table. We were all working out similar pathologies.

My need for self-discovery and acceptance was being masked by negative and dangerous behaviors. My behaviors were also a way of hiding. Because of how I was raised to view homosexuality, my personal beliefs were totally at odds with my church teachings. Even thinking about pursuing a same-sex relationship was taboo in my religious tradition. So, within the relationships that I pursued was a subliminal agreement to engage in deception.

Not surprisingly my friend Mike Mike deceived me. I never had any concrete proof that he was behind the robbery, but based on his actions I've always been convinced that he set events in motion. At first I didn't want to believe it. But during our argument, Mike Mike had made it clear that he saw the drugs as compensation for spending time with me. I'd refused to hand over the drugs and a few days later, armed men came to my house looking to steal from me.

In the aftermath of the shooting, I struggled to uncover the reasons why I'd refused to allow healthy relationships or true love to enter my life. I had to finally admit that I was a person who ran from the truth. But the truth is what sets you free. If you want to become free the only choice is to tell the truth. Whether it's distorted or seems backward or is simply too painful to speak out loud, the truth must be brought to light. People hide from things they don't want to admit about themselves. We wear masks because we believe our masks will cause us to be more accepted in society.

But the masks that we wear are not who we really are; they're a cover-up that's based on looking good and sounding good and doing what is necessary to feel connected and included. The possibility for self-acceptance is diminished to the degree that we rely on our mask to shield us from our truths. We're never able to live fully when we're trying to people please or manage others' perceptions of us. We build our masks according to what we wish others to see and believe about us. Sometimes we try to fit into places that we aren't meant to fit in, rather than finding the places we belong, the places that our souls are calling for us to enter.

Society, culture, and organized religion are some of the structures that dictate how we build our masks. Our jobs, friends and families also dictate the different levels and layers that we add to our masks. But when people make their life choices from a duplicitous state of being, the ramifications are far reaching. You never know what will happen. People lose their power and authenticity. People lose their families and friends. They end up on drugs. They land in prison. They lose jobs and homes and marriages. The fastest way to negative consequences is by refusing to be true to yourself.

Trying to manage the fallout that inevitably comes from making poor choices leads us to adopt a host of coping mechanisms. Embracing the mask means living a lie. This was definitely what happened in my case. For the longest time, I lived a lie. The fact that I was shot in the head makes sense on the symbolic level because for years I'd been trying to hide my real identity and the head is what most people consider to be the source of identity. We identify ourselves by our minds, our brains—how we think about who we are. It is the seat of consciousness. Being shot in the head is spiritually symbolic of the old identity dying and a new identity being reborn;

only when I was reborn in consciousness could I wake up to the truth of who I am.

It was miraculous for me to get to that place of being reborn. My mask was off. For the first time I gained a level of self-acceptance independent of circumstances or the beliefs of others. My life began to move forward rather than being stagnated or heading backwards. I was no longer caught up in a downward spiral that had me seeking love in dangerous places. I wasn't trying to please people anymore. And I didn't attract the type of friends who wanted to use me to further their own agenda. I finally resolved to let go of that which no longer served me. It was freeing to admit that my own choices had been blocking me and not allowing me to live up to my full potential. From a purely spiritual perspective, the boy that shot me did me a favor because it was through those events that I finally became present to my truth.

Whenever we have negative experiences in our lives, we must struggle to remember that it's never about the people who seek to do us harm. There's always something more that we can consider; a lesson to be learned, a truth that is waiting to be revealed. The circumstances and situations that surround us are always about what's going on inside us. Most people don't experience something as dramatic as being shot in the head. But the process is still the same. We're being asked to remove the mask and face the truth about the ways in which we're being called to grow and change.

Stop hiding from the things that you think make you

different. Instead, just name them. You can say things like, "I don't like the fact that I don't fit in with my family." "I don't like it when I lie to people I care about." "I'm afraid I'll never be loved if people see who I really am." "I cheat on my wife." Stop hiding from the things you fear most or making excuses for why you haven't addressed these things before. We must be willing to name the fears, beliefs and actions that cause us harm before we can change them.

Nothing happens by chance and there are consequences for refusing to heed the call that has been placed on each of our lives. The voice of the ego tells us that our selfish behaviors are all right, but the voice of Spirit lets us know in no uncertain terms that it's not. Contrary to what some people believe, the voice of Spirit (or God) isn't punishing us for not listening. Rather, we all experience the cause-and-effect consequences of our behaviors.

It can be hard to admit to our shortcomings. Some people want to stay in darkness and continue to hide. They become afraid when they hear you trying to tell your truth. But it must be done. So find a safe space to share your story. Whether you speak with a mentor, best friend, therapist, pastor or support group, find someone you trust that can hear your experiences. Ask this person to hold the high watch for you and all that you've overcome. If you speak with a friend or relative make sure he or she is someone who knows how to maintain your confidence and won't use what you say to later desecrate your character. Unfortunately, opening up to the wrong people can make us afraid to open up in the future.

We grow spiritually sicker and sicker with each negative secret we keep. But verbally telling our story may be too difficult for some people in the beginning. So writing about it may be the better option. Writing is another key that unlocks the spaces inside us that lead to change and growth. Tell your story and when you get to the part that you've played in creating pain or drama, don't shy away from it. Keep going and write until there's nothing left to say. Write unto you get to the core of the problem. The goal here is to take full responsibility for your part in the conflicts in your life, your growing edge. That's the only part that you have any control or responsibility for anyway. Other people must deal with their own actions, beliefs and consequences.

Going through this process helped me stop blaming others for my experiences. Instead, I concentrated only on what I needed to own and what I had learned from the situation. Initially this was very difficult to do. My ego didn't want to be exposed. But the truth had to be exposed in order for me to go to the next level. If you allow your ego to run your life you'll never be able to make the higher choice. Other people and their actions will always have power over the quality and the outcomes of your reality.

After you name it, say it out loud and write it down, it's time to make restitution. Pray for strength and understand that if you've harmed another person, you'll have to address that injury. You can't just clear your side of the street. Find a way to make meaningful amends for the part that you played in any painful situation.

Once you do that you're clear to let it go. Oftentimes people are their own worst enemy, their most unforgiving critic. When we feel that we've hurt people it can be very difficult to forgive ourselves for whatever we perceive as our wrongdoing. Sometimes even the person who's been wronged releases the situation long before we do. But self-forgiveness must occur if we're ever to embrace a new path. Self-forgiveness allows us to keep the lessons we've learned while releasing the baggage that comes along with that lesson.

It's extremely important to get insight into how we behave when we're not in spiritual alignment with our good. That way when those behaviors arise we're less likely to blame other people, projecting our fears and insecurities outward. We can own our humanness. That's when we have the power to make the better choice and get in alignment with our true values.

Mindfulness is crucial in this process so that we can recognize these habits and patterns as they arise, rather than afterwards. Prayer and meditation are the most powerful keys to being able to do this. Pray for guidance in whatever way makes the most sense to you. The Scripture says in Matthew 6:33 *But seek ye first the kingdom of God and his righteousness and all things will be added unto you.* (NKJV) My personal prayer is *look to the hills from which your help comes.* To me this means don't try to figure it out yourself. Let go and let God be the source of your deliverance.

Scripture also says in Romans 12:2b, *Be ye transformed by the renewing of your mind.* (NKJV)When we look to a higher

47

source for help, our minds can be opened to insight and inspiration. Through prayer and meditation the awareness of God shows up. The right path will open before us; following that path will lead to right consequences. Going down the wrong path brings about more negative consequences. Right consequences will allow you to be of benefit to others, to show them how to come up out of their trials and hardships. That's why you come out of the darkness—not just for yourself, but for those coming behind you. We call that service.

We all have work to do to clear away the mental and emotional garbage that blocks us from reaching our highest potential. When you make choices that are in alignment with your true nature, you start getting clear instructions from Spirit on the best ways to master your work and attain your goals. Life becomes simpler. You get respect from people who before didn't want to see you coming. Being in alignment will allow you to accomplish your dreams and then move forward to focus on bigger, loftier dreams.

I defied the expectations of doctors, social workers, family and friends who said someone with permanent brain damage would never be able to function as well as an able-bodied person. Yet, I went on to earn two masters degrees and become an ordained minister. God used me to show others that we can choose to make the impossible possible. And my life continues to unfold. The sky is the limit and I am free to create the life of my choosing, rather than suffer through a life that was chosen for me.

Freedom is one of the most important things that you can possibly experience. Doing this work frees you from the bondage of wrong thinking and consequences of repeatedly making bad choices. There's no longer a need to hide or pretend for the benefit of others. That's what freedom is all about: embracing the choice to be you, just as you are, without making excuses. Becoming spiritually free dispels the fear that chained us to our masks in the first place.

Before I started my journey I was so afraid to be true to myself. I feared being kicked out of my church home and abandoned by my friends and family. But none of those fears were real. I came to understand that I'd mentally and emotionally left the church long before the church could leave me. I had already abandoned my family before they could abandon me. I was the author of my own pain because I'd refused to stand up for what I believed to be right.

Today I live in freedom. When you live in freedom you get to love yourself and others unconditionally. You get to know that people are in your life because they're meant to be and that there are no mistakes. God created us all in the same perfect image and likeness. As we become free, we're able to honor that perfection in others, rather than trying to change people into who we believe that they should be. Freedom means getting to choose anew every day to be all that God intended.

Reflections

I related to...

_____

_____

_____

_____

_____

_____

_____

_____

_____

_____

_____

_____

_____

CHAPTER THREE

There are No Mistakes:
Releasing mental blocks and old
beliefs to embrace new options

When I was growing up my father would tell me that I was a mistake. Though he always claimed to be "joking," he repeatedly declared, "Mark, you weren't supposed to be born." I understood that I had not been a planned pregnancy. But even as a child I recognized that being unplanned is very different than being unwanted. My father was letting me know that I was unwanted. These beliefs lay the foundation for my understanding of myself: that I was a deadbeat, a beggar, a bum, a mistake, unwanted and unloved, at least by my father and grandfather. Embracing these false beliefs eventually led me to make some worst choices in my life.

If my father became frustrated with me for any reason, he would say things like, "The more I try to teach you, the dumber I get." So I began to believe that I couldn't learn as fast or as well as others. However, when we'd go out into the community (especially into the liquor houses that my father liked to frequent) he would brag about me to other people. He'd tell everyone we met that I was his son and how gifted I was and how he was so proud of my talents. I glowed with pride from his praise, but his kind words outside didn't prevent him from being verbally and physically abusive inside our home.

My father gave me disgraceful beatings. He would make me take my clothes off and put my head between his legs and he would beat me with switches and straps. This happened on a regular basis. One time, when I was about eight-years-old he gave me such a brutal beating that he scarred my genitals, causing permanent damage. But the psychological damage that my father caused far outlasted the pain of the physical punishment.

I'd been force-fed a negative identity where my flaws and shortcomings were placed front and center. I took on these beliefs and agreed that this was the truth of my being. Not surprisingly, I became wayward and disruptive in school, where I took my frustrations out on other people. I prayed for help to come, but there was no one who could rescue me. My father had been abusive toward my mother and some of my other siblings. So they were also dealing with mental crises similar to mine. We were all suffering but no one knew how to change anything or make the situation any better.

When I was in the third grade I was taken to a mental health center to have an evaluation because of my bad behavior. The doctors wanted to diagnose me as having Attention Deficit Disorder and put me on medication. My mother refused to allow them to drug me, but I still had to go to the medical center for my counseling appointments. One day, I decided that I didn't want to go to the center. Instead I wanted to stay at home so I could play outside with my friends. My father solved the disagreement by beating me in front of all of the other kids on the playground. He beat me until I was completely disgraced in front of my friends then forced me to go to the counseling appointment.

While my story may seem especially dramatic or painful, I know that many people have been through similar situations. People who've survived abuse of any kind tend to keep their masks on, so that others won't see what they've been through. However, abuse leaves an indelible mark; it affects who we believe that we are and tells us what we do (or don't) deserve to experience in life. Believing in a negative self-image, no matter where it originates, dramatically decreases our sense of personal wellbeing.

Humans are social creatures who crave connection; we will do anything to feel loved, wanted and accepted. As a counselor, I worked with many young men who had similar experiences to mine. I saw that they acted out in many of the same ways that I did when I was young. Some became bullies. Others dropped out of school or were chronically truant. Some of the boys went as far as to join gangs so they could feel like they were in control of shaping new identities for themselves. When you believe the lie, you don't try. You don't put forth the effort to expand your horizons because you've been told over and over again, in a variety of ways, that it's not possible for you.

I didn't think I could read because I had been told by family members and peers from the time I was in the second grade that I was a terrible reader. So eventually I gave up. I stopped trying to get better at it and believed for many years of my life that I would never be a smart or literate person. I remember being friends with a very smart boy who always challenged me to spell new words. But I couldn't spell the words he suggested, which was incredibly disturbing to me. It hurt that I didn't feel as worthwhile or educated as my friend, even though he was younger than me. If he was able to master these simple spelling words, I should have been able to as well. To make matters worse, my well-meaning friend would often ask me questions in front of adults, which only increased my humiliation. He'd say, "Mark, spell screw. Spell hospital. Spell converse." And I couldn't.

It took me many years of trial and error to be able to read proficiently. In certain ways I was self-taught, learning to read and spell by looking at street signs or magazine covers and things like that. But I still considered myself illiterate, even after all my hard work. I didn't realize that I could actually read until I was 22-years-old and a sophomore at Morehouse College. I'd begun a new English class with a professor named Dr. Pickens, who has since passed away. At the beginning of the semester I approached Dr. Pickens and said to him (as I had said to all my previous English teachers) that I could not read and I would appreciate it if he didn't embarrass me by calling on me to read in class. Dr. Pickens replied, "Okay, Mr. Miles. Thank you very much."

After that conversation I felt confident that Dr. Pickens would keep my secret. Dr. Pickens allowed me to get comfortable in his class. Sometime in the middle of the semester, as we read the Book of James from the Bible, Dr. Pickens yelled out, "Read Mr. Miles." I couldn't believe that he'd actually done that to me. With about forty other young men in the room looking at me expectantly, I simply began to read. In that moment, a shift happened. For the first time I read without stumbling or mispronouncing any of the words. It was also the first time I understood that I was not illiterate.

The labels of "illiterate" and "uneducated" had been placed on me and I had accepted them. But they weren't true.

By rejecting those labels, I felt like I'd become a part of something wonderful. I could actually be included in the same world as these students and professors that I so admired. I finally felt like I belonged. There was an instantaneous expansion in how I identified fundamental aspects of myself.

When I was done reading I looked around the room and everything was absolutely normal. There was none of the laughing or snickering that I had experienced in high school. There was none of the judgment that I feared and that I'd previously experienced from friends and family. No one covered their faces in embarrassment or teased me afterwards for not knowing simple words. I had been challenged to change my mind about myself, and I did.

Sometimes the people who love and care for you will challenge you to re-examine your negative beliefs. Sometimes life itself will hold up the challenge for you to master. You must then make the decision whether you want to hold onto outdated beliefs or change your mind. When I was challenged, I chose not to shrink again. I chose to read, as terrifying as it was for me to expose myself in that way. When life challenges us we must decide to accept the challenge, to accept the change that comes along with moving into a different phase of life. For most people this is not an easy task. It seems extremely simple and straightforward from an intellectual standpoint. But the actual doing—making the decision move forward rather than shying away—can be extremely difficult.

Sometimes we know that an action is damaging, but we do it anyway. We feel blocked, for whatever reason, from pursuing what's in our best interest. Patterns, habits and beliefs can block you even when you consciously know that they're detrimental. Fear of failing and fear of success are also powerful blockages to our greatness. We all want to embrace our spiritual truth. We want to stop believing the lies that we've been told about ourselves. Fortunately, there are many tools that we can use to help release these stubborn beliefs and allow our innate power to shine through.

One of my favorite tools is positive affirmation. In order to raise our self-esteem we must find creative ways to reprogram our conscious and subconscious mind. Making a practice of using positive affirmation is one of the ways to counter the false beliefs that threaten to overwhelm us. *I think therefore I am. I am the master of my fate and the captain of my soul.* We get to speak our truth over and over again as we retrain our minds to follow a higher path. We speak our truth until we begin to believe it.

As a man thinketh so is he. Hold fast to the truth that the brilliance and beauty and vision waiting to be tapped from within you are more powerful than anything you've ever known. That is true of us all. And we must do whatever it takes to bring our awareness into alignment with the truth. You were meant to be here. Look back at your record. Look at all of the times when you've brought your gifts to bear for others and to raise yourself out of conflict or painful situations. Look at the responses that you receive from others when you share your gifts.

When I sing at events I get standing ovations. For a long time, being on stage was the only time that I felt validated. But it was enough to help me change my mind about what I was capable of expressing. Using that platform helped me move forward to a more expansive platform of self-awareness and discovery. It helped me to remind myself of everything that I'd done right, rather than constantly replaying mental pictures of what I'd done wrong.

The light within you is powerful and bright. But you must claim it to set it free. Affirming the truth is one way to lay claim to it and bring it forth. When using positive affirmations it helps to write them down and post them anywhere that you can see them. This is something that most spiritual teachers suggest in order to receive the greatest benefit from this practice. Leave notes to yourself in your car or on your bathroom mirror or anywhere that you will see them at various points in the day. When I took baths I would soothe myself with candles and meditation music and I'd post my affirmations where I could read them in that relaxed state. I would reflect and meditate on the things that I had written down, not just reading them by rote (and becoming desensitized to their message).

Be consistent with the practice of thinking and speaking

positively to yourself. The same is true of using affirmative prayer to affect change in your life. At its heart, prayer is an affirmation of your true nature, your connection to God and what you want to see manifest in your life and the world. So open yourself to the incredible effects of prayer. Surround yourself with people who will undertake this practice with you and who are committed to their own betterment.

Pray and then open your heart with great expectancy and anticipation to receive your help, your answered prayer. The answers may not come in the form that you would've expected or even hoped for. They may not come when you think you should receive them, but they will come. The shift will happen. Continue to remind yourself to look to the hills. This is a practice of repetition. Through repetitive insistence on seeing and receiving your good, you are retraining your mind to accept that which you want to experience, rather than focusing on (and receiving) more of what brings you pain.

Another step to releasing mental blocks is to journal about the pain or confusion or damage that you feel has been done to you. Then write in your journal about the solutions that you wish to experience. Keep writing until you find doors opening for you and your life changing to reflect what you've called forth with your words. Make the choice to believe in yourself, to hold your head up. Writing about your experiences can give you the strength to own the things that have happened to you without blaming yourself for them. It gives you perspective.

As you're doing this spiritual work, remind yourself that your efforts are enough. "It is enough," is a very powerful statement. It's powerful in its simplicity and its radical acceptance, which is necessary when you're trying to change your mind and your life. Self-acceptance provides the spirit of God the space to step in and redirect your path. You can't re-create your life solely using your own power. God must stand in partnership. You get to claim and affirm that this process of change is happening *now*. It's not something that will happen sometime off in the future after you become worthy. Only in the present moment is it possible to come into agreement with the change that you seek and then allow it to manifest.

The art of allowing is an extremely important step that often gets overlooked. Allowing is part of a spiritual practice, which is based in release and surrender. The spirit of God wants to be expressed through us. When we allow His spirit to come through us without judgment or hesitation, we become open to far greater gifts than we've ever imagined. To do this we must let go of our attachment to what we think answered prayer should look, feel or sound like. Instead, we surrender in the knowledge that whatever is happening is ultimately for our greater good and for the good of others.

In other words, allowing means getting out of our own way and being open-minded. At this point there's no action to be taken. We are deep into the process of surrendering. Surrender is a profound spiritual principle as well. Many people often misunderstand what it means to surrender in the spiritual sense. In a worldly context, surrender means to give up or give in. But to surrender in a spiritual sense mean giving up your insistence on fighting. You're not fighting yourself or other people anymore. You're not fighting outcomes anymore. You accept all aspects of life, positive and negative, as they are. You allow yourself to embrace reality without fear or judgment, rather than wishing it away. I've witnessed people I love seeming to go down the wrong path and I've had to practice the art of surrender. I know that, no matter what the situation looks like, the best possible outcome is working out for the people I love and all those surrounding them.

Surrendering also mean releasing the need to change the thoughts and opinions of others. When someone has opinions about you, good or bad, you don't take those opinions as truth. You recognize them for what they are, namely someone else's beliefs. As the old saying goes, what people say or believe about you is really none of your business. The only thing that's of concern to you is what you say and believe about yourself. Life is so much simpler, sweeter and more peaceful when we stop fighting the world and simply let go and let God. Take your hands off of the situation. Then you can peacefully agree to disagree with others who don't share your point of view. Nothing is taken away from either of you. You need not make yourself (or anyone else) wrong. There's great freedom in having the ability to bear witness to circumstances without seeking to control or manipulate them.

When you use these practices repeatedly, you begin to see new options taking shape for yourself. You step out of the old limitations and into a new identity with incredible opportunities available to you that may have seemed impossible before. You can pick up where you left off in any unsuccessful previous attempts at self-improvement. That might mean going back to school or getting a better job or reconnecting with your family. You'll see things differently from this vantage point. And the things you thought you wanted might change, too.

It wasn't until after I was shot that I decided to go back to school for my first Masters degree in mental health counseling. Doing such a thing would never have occurred to me in my other life. But I became present to so many new ways of helping others because of the trauma that I experienced. Through my studies I learned how to identify behaviors and disorders that had affected me and so many other people. More importantly, I learned strategies to help with the healing process. In looking to heal others, I learned how to heal myself.

Allow your spirit to guide you in new directions and occupations. Your soul knows where it wants to go. No longer will you be tempted to look towards society's dictates or to other people for your validation. Instead, look within to the wisdom and resources of your own soul. You have new lens. We never know what gifts life has to offer us. So, changing our minds also means opening our minds to what is beyond our current ability to comprehend. Open your mind to see the best that God has to offer you. Open your mind to the unknown.

Oftentimes, people insist that the unknown is scary. But there's another perspective that holds the unknown as a path to liberation. The Call lies in the unknown. Your life assignment lies in the unknown. Changing and opening your mind to new possibilities puts you into the flow of God. The flow is like a peaceful stream with no upset or turbulence. There's just an opening. In the flow, we experience right action and right direction and right seeing. The way becomes straight. Healing is demonstrated in the areas of your life where pain has dominated. When the flow stops, struggle begins. All too often, rather than becoming steppingstones, our struggles stop us and block us from continuing in the right direction. But when we allow ourselves to change our minds and set out on a new path, clarity arises from confusion.

Of course, this is an ongoing process. Change is always occurring, as well as our challenge to embrace these changes. We crave steadiness, stability and comfort because change can be interpreted as a direct threat to our wellbeing. But we must get comfortable with being uncomfortable if we are to master the art of changing our minds. Rather than trying to know everything, we must surrender, trust, and believe. Change is about paradigm shifts. If you're going to be in alignment with where your soul is going, you must step into that shift. It's the only way to embrace life's pruning process and come out on the other side of the change restored.

Reflections

I related to...

CHAPTER FOUR

What Must Be Done: Following through
on the spiritual truth about you

Learning to follow through on the spiritual truths that we've been discussing is one of the most important aspects of this journey. Oftentimes people hear spiritual teachings that shake them to the core. They experience epiphanies or spiritual awakenings and feel as though they are changed forever. But in a short period of time, somehow life goes back to business as usual. They may agree wholeheartedly with what they've learned. And yet they still don't follow through by acting on these principles to make substantial and lasting changes. In other words, they don't actually *do* anything that will alter their circumstances to help them to make a permanent shift.

For most of us, change is hard. In fact many people experience change as not just hard but virtually impossible. You may have been trying to lose weight for five or ten years and still haven't lost a pound. Or you want to make more money but your bank balance stays in the red. Or you keep talking about going back to school but you've never gotten your degree. No matter the situation, the experience remains the same: life continues to pass on by but the real breakthroughs always seem just out of reach.

That feeling of stagnation can be one of the most devastating experiences to come to terms with. It's the nagging idea, which says, "I feel as though I am wasting my life." No matter what examples, exercises or spiritual principles we may learn, it's still each person's individual choice and responsibility to follow through with applying the information to reshape his or her world. We must each discover for ourselves the right action steps to take.

We get to choose if we're actually going to do whatever it takes to embrace change or if we'll follow the road of what's most popular in any given situation. We must choose whether we'll do what's comfortable or uncomfortable, what is expedient or what is right. We get the biggest results when we're willing to be uncomfortable in the pursuit of change and growth. While it's true that some people do experience change as easy, comfortable and graceful, for many of us change requires letting go of our preconceived ideas about reality. And that's hard.

Embracing change, standing up for yourself—for the things that you know to be right and just—can be frightening. People often fear being confronted with past mistakes or things they could have done better. They also fear confronting others about perceived injustices. It's just easier to maintain the status quo. But unless we push through we'll remain energetically stagnant. Moreover, we'll continue to experience lack in important areas of our lives because everything is interconnected. But when we boldly step out on faith, our actions come into alignment with our highest good. We also become a benefit to others in our communities and families.

I experienced this firsthand when I initially entered college. Because of my poor academic record I wasn't a good candidate for my first choice school, Morehouse College. I had to start at a smaller, less prestigious school. So I attended a local college in South Carolina. The school was an overwhelmingly uncompromising institution of higher learning where in my view the few students of color weren't necessarily always made to feel welcome. While I was there I was elected president of the Black Student's Fellowship Organization on campus. One day, some students from my organization came to me to report that they were being harassed by the administration. These young African-American men lived in a neighboring dorm and were star athletes who played basketball for the college.

The boys had been besieged with rumors that they were doing drugs and drinking on campus, which was completely against the regulations of this religious school. There had been no proof to support these allegations until a wine bottle mysteriously appeared during a dorm search of two of the young men. I was present in the room when administrators from the Student Association "discovered" the bottle. I immediately asked to see it, too, and noticed there were blonde hairs wrapped around it.

It didn't make sense that there would be blonde hairs on a bottle of alcohol supposedly being consumed by two young black men. I said as much and insisted that the whole situation was a set up. There were about 20 athletes in the dorm who had experienced this kind of treatment and whose academic careers were on the line. But the two who had the alcohol planted in their room were now in danger of being immediately expelled. I maintained that their treatment was pure bias and it was wrong. That caused the administrator's attention to shift from the athletes to me.

The harassment started immediately. Student Association administrators insisted that I do manual labor, cutting leaves and cleaning up behind the classroom buildings in a swampy area that students were never asked to go into under any circumstances. They demanded that I start cleaning trash otherwise I would be suspended.

I was forced to hide from S.A. administrators on multiple occasions in my friends' dorm rooms. I knew that they were trying to have me expelled from school under the grounds of "insubordination." So I was convinced that any run-ins with those men would not end well for me. It got to the point where I had to hide under my own bed when they came banging on my door in the middle of the night.

They upped the ante again by reporting me to the police multiple times. If they could have me removed from the campus during the night when the school offices were closed I would have no recourse, no one to intercede on my behalf. Not knowing what else to do, I showed up at the president's door at 10 p.m. one night and asked him if he would please do something to stop the harassment from the S.A. administrators. He couldn't (or wouldn't) intercede.

By this point, there was only a week of school left, finals week. To leave before the end of finals would mean that I'd receive failing grades in all of my classes, destroying any chance that I had to transfer into Morehouse College. I needed to somehow maintain the presence of mind to follow through on what I had started—to do what needed to be done. The fear and the anger and the stress felt overwhelming. I simply couldn't figure out how to help the young men who were relying on me or how to help myself. The university had all the power. Or so it seemed. Although the situation appeared hopeless, I was being called to change, to grow beyond my present paradigm. Spirit was asking me to stand with unshakable faith in my beliefs, to do what was right no matter the outcome.

I prayed, listening for direction and guidance, ready to act on whatever it was that I heard. The still, small voice within gave me the unmistakable command to ask for help. Asking for help was not easy for me. But I had to follow through with the directive no matter how difficult it seemed. I knew that I was being led in the right direction. The psalmist says, *He leadeth me in the path of righteousness.* To me that is a literal spiritual truth. But we must ask for—and heed—His guidance.

The direction to ask for help led me to call the NAACP. I appealed to NAACP investigators who picked up the case. They arrived at the college quickly, intent on doing their own investigation. The involvement of the NAACP investigators was the key to finally ending the persecution for the athletes, who were able to maintain their status as students. The findings from the biased room search were dismissed. It remained to be seen, however, whether I would be allowed to complete my school year. Again, I prayed over the outcome. As I prayed, God lifted the fear, doubt and worry from my shoulders. The certainty that I would be vindicated washed over me.

The next day, I entered into the Dean's office to discuss the situation. Rather than being overcome with fear, I sat down in front of the man filled with calm and peace. The Dean asked me, "What would you think we should do about your situation?" I replied, "You can do whatever you want to do. God has already told me that I'm good. He already gave me the answer."

Something touched the Dean's heart that day. He forgave the entire situation and declared that no further action was to be taken against me. With this weight off my shoulders, I was able to make it through the last few of days of the semester. In fact, once my finals were completed and it was time for me to leave campus, the Dean actually gave me $10 in gas money to get home. He was a righteous man who helped me turn a terrible situation into something positive.

Being willing to listen and then take action on the guidance that I was being given allowed me to see my hard work finally bear fruit. But most importantly, it put me in the right position to take the next big step in my life. Moreover, I now had a testimony, as well as a much greater understanding of my own ability to be a leader. In the end the experience was an incredible blessing. After teaming with the NAACP investigators and seeing how their dedicated work changed the lives of so many, I was led to write a letter to the admissions team at Morehouse.

I explained to them why I would be a good candidate to attend their school and I spoke of the experience with the NAACP and what I'd learned. When the Dean at Morehouse read my letter he was stunned. He couldn't believe that I had been through such an experience and I'm sure that it swayed him as he considered whether or not to invite me to be a student. The Dean then asked me to audition for the chairman of the music department, which was led by Dr. Wendell Phillips Whalum Sr.

I arrived at the audition nervous and worried about making the cut. But, again, I prayed for guidance and to be led on the path of right action. My job was simply to follow through, to make myself available to the Spirit of God that was seeking to move through me. After Dr. Whalum heard me sing he asked, "Why didn't you apply to Morehouse sooner?" I replied, "I didn't apply sooner because I didn't feel that I was good enough." He said, "Mark, you should have your butt whooped. You should have been here." It was a big deal for me. Having the honor of being the last student, actually recruited by Dr. Whalum was overwhelming enough! But now actually singing in the world renowned Morehouse College Glee Club, totally knocked me off my feet! It took weeks before I could even open my mouth to sing a singular note. It was the first time I had ever heard an all-African American male chorus, sing fluidly and by memory music of all genres including a foreign language. I recall vividly Dr. Morrow snapping me out of it during rehearsal by yelling, "Sing Mark Miles!"

Not only was I accepted, but I was accepted with a scholarship and placed into the honors dorm. The fact that I had followed through on guidance given to me during a time of hardship allowed me to be where I wanted to be and put me there under circumstances better than I ever could have hoped for on my own. Following through is key. It is a critical part of the process, even when you're not sure of the outcome. You must be willing to do your part.

Doing your part means taking the appropriate actions steps toward your goals, listening to guidance and knowing what you're bringing to the table. If you don't identify what you are bringing to the table you could be stopped by your own feelings of unworthiness. You could believe the lie that you have nothing of value to contribute. But you do. Everyone has his or her own unique gifts and talents to share. To find your path toward actualizing those talents you must recognize what works for you, even if it's not conventional. I wouldn't have been able to get into Morehouse College by taking the same route as the majority of other students. I had to find a different door.

We each have our own doors to walk through. And if we can't find an open door there will be a window. Sometimes we have to go around to the side. But there will be a way. If the path toward a goal isn't smooth and straight it can be easy to believe, "Oh, this thing that I wanted must not really be for me." And that's when we give up. But that's the time to recommit and go further, to affirm in thought, word and deed that what we want can be ours.

People don't understand how powerful their word is and how setting a strong intention is all that it takes to set the wheels in motion of change into your life. Ultimately, you get to say whether your dreams and goals will manifest. Most people don't understand how pivotal setting intentions can be. If you set specific intentions for your life, the way to actualize those intentions will show up, though it may be completely different than the traditional route. But don't be fooled. The path has already been laid out before you.

There are hurdles, but you have the strength and the stamina to jump over or go around them. You can say to this mountain, "move, get out of my way," and the mountain will move. The way will be made. You are that powerful. When we speak our heartfelt truths and desires, it is the I Am who is speaking through us. Whatever we attach to those words will manifest through our actions. We must learn to speak of ourselves and our circumstances in ways that are in alignment with what we wish to see.

I am great. I am magnificent. I am extraordinary. I am confident. I am capable. Knowing the spiritual truth about yourself brings completely different results than giving in to the fears of the ego by saying things like, *I am stupid… I am dumb… I am just an addict... I am never going to be able to create the life that I want...* The "I Am" determines the outcome that will ultimately unfold before you. We get stopped when we restrict God's infinite capabilities with our finite mindset and beliefs. We may subconsciously feel safer mimicking the limitations that have been placed on us, but ultimately we get to set the parameters of our own worth.

Setting these parameters too small puts you in the position of trying to do it all yourself, which always invites more hardship and struggle. And if you try to cheat or get over on others to make your journey easier, you better believe that struggle will still show up to mirror your consciousness. Standing in right action, however, begins with stating your needs clearly to yourself, to God and to others. If you're trying to go to school, for example, but you don't have the money to pay for it you must speak your needs clearly to the people who can help you. That's very different than just throwing up your hands and saying, "Ah, woe is me. I can't afford college." For the person who's able to humbly assert that they need help, help will be given.

I've been in the position where I had to say, "I need $25,000 to complete this year of school and I have no idea where it will come from." But I stayed open, knowing that I'd be able to complete my education. And the money showed up. Now, most of the money showed up in the form of student loans, which at the time I did not have the means to repay. But the grace of God doesn't stop there. In my case, after racking up nearly a quarter of a million dollars in student loans for three degrees, I ultimately had the majority of those loans forgiven through means that others would have said were impossible. But nothing is impossible with God.

In our Western society we're taught that we must do everything on our own. If you need help you're weak, a taker, someone who doesn't deserve the compassion of others. This is a lie. People who are most successful allow others to help them when needed as they, in turn, regularly help others through the generosity of their own spirit. It's reciprocity.

Very few of us pull ourselves up by our own bootstraps, no matter what we're told. We're surrounded and assisted by others willing to take part in our quest to realize our goals. I had a dean at Morehouse, a man named Dean Hudson, who was an incredible inspiration to me throughout my career at the school. At one point, I was on the verge of finishing up my undergraduate degree after many years of work and setbacks. But I had run out of money at the end of the final semester.

Not knowing what else to do, I turned to Dean Hudson for help. He made certain that I received a scholarship that covered my graduation expenses, my cap and gown and my class ring, with enough money left over to buy a car. I allowed the dean to help me and, in return, I gave him what he asked me for: grades. I made sure that my end-of-semester grades were above and beyond the requirements for the scholarship that I received. But it never would've happened if I hadn't been honest about what I was going through.

Being honest doesn't mean you're begging or being needy. Again, we're all here to be each other's support system in times of trouble. *No man is an island. No man stands alone. Each man as my brother, each man as my friend.* We need one another. And we have the opportunity to change our minds about believing the lie that we don't. There's nothing wrong with us for reaching out and allowing people into our lives to enrich us. We are meant to be interconnected.

If you want to hurt someone, put that person in isolation. Humans don't do well when we're separated from each other.

We are happiest in community. But when we don't develop our gifts because we've refused to ask for help, we stunt ourselves. We also make it harder for others to journey down their own path. We are denying them both our assistance and our example. That's when we become takers: when we take back our gifts and talents and hide them from the light.

However, when we take action on behalf of others, we ultimately move ourselves much further down our own path than we could ever have dreamed. I received my greatest wish (to attend Morehouse College) in large part through helping a group of talented young men further their dreams and goals. The circle continues to spiral ever upward. That's what people mean by the phrase "paying it forward." We become each other's eyes and ears walking through the world, looking for ways to assist.

We need to get that. We are not each other's enemies. The belief in scarcity and competition is a sociological construct built on insecurity. We were born as brothers and sisters, meant to live in love and harmony. When you let others help you on your journey they may bring you a piece of your own puzzle that you didn't have before, which allows you to make the final steps towards your goal. You never know what blessings people will bring into your life or what lessons they have come to teach you.

Learning always goes both ways. That is the truth in every facet of life. The students teach the teachers. The employees teach managers. The husband teaches the wife and the wife teaches the husband. The church members teach the preacher.

Reciprocity is necessary if we want to build communities that are thriving and not dying. We die emotionally and spiritually when we live in fear of supporting or helping one another.

People who are walking through the world asleep will routinely try to destroy, criminalize or marginalize other people. The sleepwalkers hold the mistaken belief that if someone else is taking action to meet his or her needs, then there won't be enough left for them. So they try to stop other people from achieving. But we're all unstoppable, made in the image and likeness of God. Though it often seems that human beings have been a disruptive force on the planet, the reality is that we are all creators of the highest order.

Unfortunately, some of us create disaster everywhere we go because we don't know who we are. But when we choose instead to create harmony and love, that's when we're living at our fullest potential. Look at your actions on moment-by-moment basis and ask yourself, *what am I creating here? Am I following through on something that will bring life and joy and fulfillment and beauty to others? Are my actions benefiting the whole? Are my intentions meant to break others down or build them up?*

We're talking about living consciously, not just walking through life being oblivious to the effects of your actions. We want to create our lives with a strong intention for what we want to see manifest in our communities and the world at large. Then our actions have meaning and the effects of those actions can benefit others for generations to come.

Reflections

I related to...

CHAPTER FIVE

Prophetic Voice vs. Pathetic Voice:
Making the big paradigm shift

Alive inside each of us are two disparate voices. The first is what I call the prophetic voice, or the voice of Spirit. The second is the pathetic voice, the voice of the ego. As the ego's mouthpiece, the pathetic voice only sees what's wrong—what you can't do, what's missing from your life. It is the voice that tries to keep you small and afraid of moving through the obstacles in your path. The pathetic voice is also disruptive. It prevents you from owning the truth of any situation, which would require you to grow. Instead the pathetic voice denies reality, acting out in anger and refusing to take responsibility for the outcomes of its' actions.

I first became aware of these two voices in the months after I was shot. My recovery process proved to be a long, slow road. When I lost my cognitive abilities it impacted every area of my life, including my finances. Within two years I was on the verge of losing my home. I was unable to work the way I used to, but my responsibilities continued to grow. I felt afraid and had no idea how to adjust to this new reality.

My counseling position at the middle school had ended. Though I still had benefits from that job, I no longer had the income. Subsequently I moved back to South Carolina where I'd purchased a home, thinking that I'd be able to get back to work as quickly as possible despite my new disabilities. Long-term disability and Social Security benefits covered my expenses initially. But as my financial outlook became increasingly dire I begin to lose faith. I even moved out of my home and put a renter into the property to offset costs. But I still found it difficult to juggle the mounting bills.

Desperate for a change and to have some forward motion, I decided to go back to school. This time I moved from South Carolina to Atlanta, Georgia. But when I decided to go back to Atlanta the cost-of-living increase meant that my money wouldn't stretch as far anymore. The house payment combined with my apartment rent combined with my school schedule and therapy commitments became overwhelming. The pathetic voice was constantly in my head spewing fear and doubt: *You really can't make these payments. You're going to lose your house and you don't want to lose your house so what are you going to do? You don't have the money to pay. If you lose your house then your renter, your relative, is going to be out on the street and will be all your fault!*

Despite my best efforts, I continued to fall further and further behind in my mortgage payments. It was very difficult for me to manage the money that I was receiving in rent to keep up with the mortgage. Sadly, I didn't always use that money to pay the house note. Sometimes I bought books that I needed for school. At other times I used the money for my own living expenses so that I could keep my head above water.

All the while, the pathetic voice kept rearing its ugly head because I was out of integrity. Constant anxiety, worry and doubt kept me in fear of having everything topple down around me. I didn't believe that I'd be able to matriculate through school while keeping my house and my financial head above water. *How will all this look?* I wondered. *What will my family and friends think of me? What did I think of myself?* The pathetic voice was baiting me with these thoughts, keeping me overly concerned with other people's judgments and opinions.

Because the pathetic voice is also a people pleasing voice, it wanted to convince me to focus on appearances rather than owning my truth and finding real solutions. It wanted to look good and there was no way that I could continue to look good if the people I cared about discovered that I was doing so poorly. I lived in fear of being embarrassed and shamed.

The situation continued to spiral out of control until I became conscious of the fact that I was taking part in my own demise by listening to this voice of victimhood. The circumstances appeared dire, yes, but it was still within my power to choose which thoughts to give my energy. I decided to make a different choice. I began to listen deeply and attentively for the voice that I now call the prophetic voice.

This is the voice of Spirit that said over and over again in Isaiah 54:17, *No weapon formed against you shall prosper.* (NKJV) It was the voice of peace that told me to stop worrying and, instead, go to God in prayer. So I did. Whenever the familiar anxiety began to creep over me, rather than giving in to panic I prayed. One day, while I was in prayer, I received very specific guidance. I was directed to talk to the bankers in charge of my loan and discuss the possibility of having the loan modified. It seemed like a long shot, but the prophetic voice was so clear and so certain that I knew I had to listen— no matter what the outcome.

It was a daunting process to release the pathetic voice. But it was also a life-changing discovery to realize that the pathetic voice wasn't really me. Or, more correctly, it was not representative of my higher self. Most people identify with their thoughts and beliefs, never challenging them to understand where those thoughts come from. They never stop to question if they *really* believe what their inner voice is saying when it speaks of fear and lack and unworthiness.

The prophetic voice, on the other hand, is always speaking, too. It's just waiting for a listening ear. It is the voice of hope and light, the voice that doesn't give in to worry. It affirms that you're doing the best that you can in any given moment and that everything will work together for your good in the end. It's the voice that admonishes us to tell the truth, to be honest and upfront about what's going on in our lives instead of trying to hide or manipulate circumstances.

The prophetic voice asks us to embrace our vulnerability rather than wallow in shame, worrying about being "found out" for our shortcomings. Our power lies in accessing this voice because once we do we realize that there's no need for worry. Worry is simply a lack of faith. When our faith in our connection to Spirit is strong, there's no need to be overly concerned about other people's opinions or agonize over the challenges that we face. Faith dissolves the worry. When I stopped focusing on what others thought of me and stopped believing that people were out to get me, the prophetic voice became clearer and stronger in my mind.

Giving up my addiction to listening to the pathetic voice wasn't easy. It's not easy for most people. But I began to look at each choice I made and discern where that choice had originated. The choices that originated from the prophetic voice guided me down the road of peace and security. For example, after being led to speak to the loan officers I was able to secure a loan modification that saved my house and prevented me from going into foreclosure.

The means for saving my house seemed miraculous. I came to find out that the bank that supposedly owned the mortgage deed actually did not own it and therefore had no legal right to take the house away from me. The bank that actually held the note was willing to negotiate with me. I got a new, affordable mortgage rate, which was answered prayer. But in order to receive the insight that led to my blessings, I had to give up my addiction to worry and choose to stand in my faith. I had to have faith that the predatory loan that I had unwittingly signed could be overturned. And it was.

Going through this trying time was actually a tremendous blessing for me because this was the first time that I consciously distinguished between the two voices. I've been paying attention to both voices—and the outcomes of listening to both voices—ever since. Embracing the faith-based voice meant knowing *without seeing* that everything was going to be all right. The voice reassured me that God was on my side. Truth was on my side. Prosperity was on my side. And there were more blessings to come.

However, the pathetic voice did not just give up and slink away. It remains present always, seeking to be heard, looking for an avenue to become dominant in the consciousness again.

Being based in ego means that the pathetic voice is at the root of vanity. It wants to be right. It wants to sit in judgment. It wants to take you off course. This voice speaks defeat, because giving up will keep you small. This is the way that the ego believes it can protect you. Being small and staying the same minimizes the threat of the unknown. Its voice whispers *quit* when you are faced with any daunting task.

While the prophetic voice is the birthplace of security and abundance, the pathetic voice knows only jealousy. This energy can also show up as competition, favoritism or unsupportive behavior. Ultimately, the ego is telling you that you're not enough. Someone else is better. You don't have enough because someone else has more. And because they have more, they must do more to maintain what they have. This, of course, means that they are more capable than you. If you can't live up to those same high standards, then you have failed.

The pathetic voice knows how to get what it wants at the expense of other people and relationships. It has a way of manipulating the truth. It feeds on people's insecurities and weaknesses, like a predator. Moreover, it doesn't take responsibility for harm that it causes. Any negative outcome is someone else's fault. Suddenly, the ego becomes focused on what that person did to you and why they're wrong. But that's a delusion.

In order to stop listening to the pathetic voice and start embracing the prophetic voice, we need tools to retrain the mind and heart. Learning how to listen is key. When we're listening intently to the voice of Spirit peace shows up in our awareness. Right action and right direction follow. These fruits of the Spirit unfold in our lives with grace. This is a very different energy than the forceful influence of the ego. When you find yourself wanting to be right or wanting to make a point rather than listen, understand and exchange ideas, it's a clear sign that the pathetic voice is talking. But when we stop to listen before we speak or act, we give the prophetic voice space to make itself known. We honor the voice that speaks to and through us, that provides us with the fruits of the Spirit.

Listening, connection and empathy are anathema to the pathetic voice because it would rather find fault or blame others. It's more comfortable showing what it knows and being deferred to, rather than holding the space for others to express their truth. Choices made while listening to that voice tend to be reactions to what is going on around you, rather than measured responses to what is going on within you.

The prophetic voice leads you into the flow of right action. It can manifest as the intuition that arises in moments of quiet or meditation. Sometimes it comes as the actual words of a friend or mentor or maybe a pastor. But when you're in tune with Spirit you'll hear Its' direction within the spoken words. The path of right action has no attachment to specific outcomes and no need to hold on to struggle. It's not compelled to defend itself from those who think differently or would try to pull you from your path.

Instead, the way opens up and you walk forward, knowing that you're being led to your greater good. On this path, you understand the folly of trying to make something happen. If you're trying to force an outcome, then you can be assured that you're not moving in right action. The ego is leading your steps. Right action *allows* things and events to unfold. You may not even know exactly where you're going but it will feel "right."

Now, there's a big difference between being out of alignment and being determined to persevere through obstacles. When we persevere we release the thought of quitting from our consciousness. We know that no matter what happens, we will reach our goals with time. There's a common misunderstanding that "the universe is trying to tell you something" when you run into obstacles or face many trials. That logic says it's time to quit because you're obviously out of alignment and off track. This is when people may give up, thinking, *oh, this must not be for me.*

The challenge comes in distinguishing whether the obstacles are lessons that we need to move through with grace or if we are indeed being pushed in a different direction. Sometimes the difference between the two experiences can seem nuanced and subtle. But it's the difference between giving up on a calling verses allowing for a pause or rest period. Sometimes it's necessary to stop and regroup, to create time for reflection before moving forward once again. If you have any confusion at this kind of crossroads, simply be still. Go inward. Listen. That is when prayer, meditation and rest are indispensable.

If Spirit is actually trying to move you in a different direction, there won't be a way around the obstacles that arise. I believe that this happens because sometimes a person's wishes aren't in the best interest of his or her growth and development. That's when Spirit can help remind us to stand firm in our desire to manifest our highest intentions.

If I'm in sync with the movement of Spirit, I will grow more adept at discerning between the empathetic voice of Love and the harsh words of the ego. There's a tremendous difference in the actions and outcomes associated with each. I will know when to move and when to be still. When I'm laid low by setbacks and failures, I will know that there's also something greater that's trying to come through me and that there is another way to manifest that greatness. And in the long run, the new way of being will have more meaning and be more beneficial for all concerned.

We may need to reroute ourselves along the way to our goals so that we can find the more beneficial path. Or the timing may not be right. Again, listen and reflect on the circumstances that are showing up and what they have to tell you. Reflect on your own personal fears. They may crop up more and more the closer you come to achieving your dreams. Are you afraid of being hurt? Are you afraid of being seen differently? Are you afraid of being misunderstood?

We must always look at our own stuff on this journey and resolve to keep growing through any pain or discomfort. It's the only way to stay in alignment with our intentions. Being in alignment is standing up for the truth, being confident and refusing to be sidetracked by circumstances or our own internal fears. It means knowing that we're being divinely led, that whatever we are seeking is also seeking us.

Choosing to honor the prophetic voice over the pathetic voice is part of rich spiritual practice. Committing to this practice will change every aspect of your life. It's an integral part of a daily routine centered on prayer, meditation and affirmation. We're guided ever deeper into our sacred wisdom by doing this work. We're giving up the ego's need to do it all ourselves. There are some things that God has got to do through us. So we become still and open to God's call, limiting distractions from negatives sources and embracing harmony.

If you're not in harmony you're not in alignment. Harmony and alignment bring freedom. This kind of freedom isn't subject to the effects of the world. It cannot be limited by external chaos or drama. Even when setbacks happen, you'll be okay because you have faith that you're doing the right thing and that, with time, the doors will open to your greater good.

Time and patience are necessary to building this practice as a way of life because, as we've discussed, both voices will always be there with us. The pathetic voice will always be looking for a way to upstage the prophetic voice and get your attention. It will do anything to make itself primary once more. This is why we must stay vigilant in our conscious awareness, not allowing habits and old patterns to regain ground. That's what gives us the wisdom and strength to turn toward the voice of Spirit rather than the voice of ego on a consistent basis.

Unfortunately, so many people in the world build their lives around the voice of the ego, which tells them that in order to be worthy they must be better than others. They watch television and then mimic what they see in their own personal lives. But that is deception. Our society is, in part, based on these delusions—the lure of materialism and vanity and violence. The delusions block the gifts, talents and treasures that we were born to share from coming through. When we walk away from these delusions, we come out of the world. This is what is meant by the scriptural command to *come out from among them...* 2 Corinthians 6:17 (NKJV)

Jesus said to render unto Caesar what is his but to pursue the gifts of the Spirit. Love, charity, goodness, long-suffering, perseverance, peace and right action or self-control are all fruits of the Spirit. And the prophetic voice is the mouthpiece of the Spirit. These are the eternal qualities that we wish to focus on and multiply. While the pathetic voice asks, *what can I get?* the prophetic voice says, *what can I give?*

Of course, we can be in alignment with Spirit and listen to our prophetic voice and still have nice things. We are here to live a rich life. But we must choose which will be our master: Spirit or materialism. Giving in to materialism will have us playing an all-or-nothing game. But with Spirit, there is balance. One way to start achieving balance is by asking ourselves the question, *Who are we reaching back to serve? How are we helping and giving?* The ego will always want more. There's no satisfaction or peace in that way of being. But if our riches flow from alignment with Spirit then we can achieve not just material wealth, but also fulfillment and joy in the process.

You can acquire the things that you want without the anxiety attached to whether or not you will keep them. The things that you acquire will also have a different meaning. You'll no longer be attached to having "stuff" as a means of grasping at happiness. Nice things simply become vehicles for experiencing comfort and pleasure. The things can come or go but the experience of wellbeing is what will remain. Life ceases to be about looking or sounding good. It becomes about doing good and being good. At the highest level, life inspires you to share the good that you have—rather than seeking to horde the things that you fear could be taken away.

The path that you take makes all the difference to where you end up. Decide to seek out the voice that will undoubtedly lead you to where you want to be. The prophetic voice brings wholeness and healing into our lives. Isn't that what we all want—to heal the broken places within, to experience wholeness and peace, and to be of use to those around us? This is the hallmark of a life of fulfillment and joy. It's necessary to our experience of a life well lived.

Reflections

I related to...

CHAPTER SIX

Fear is a Racket: Letting go of
excuses and negative coping skills

Fear is one of the biggest—if not the biggest—inhibitor in the advancement of our goals. It's a primary reason that people allow themselves to be stopped in any endeavor. It's also the subtext behind our excuses as to why we're not getting where we want to be in life. Fear of failure, fear of success, fear of change, fear of staying the same—our internal anxiety can reduce us to paralysis no matter how badly we may want to move forward. When we find ourselves out of alignment, out of integrity or out of flow, fear is what usually takes over.

I know the feeling of fear intimately. I lived in fear of my father throughout my entire childhood and well into adulthood. For as long as I could remember, I endured verbal, physical, and psychological abuse from my father. We were never able to get along for any length of time. He was an alcoholic and his condition most likely exacerbated the conflict between us. But whatever the reason, our relationship was filled with intimidation and violence. The older I grew, the more the situation deteriorated.

There was always some type of upset in our family life that could be traced back to my father. He lived by the golden rule of "spare the rod and spoil the child." And he did not spare the rod. Granted, I had behaviors that needed correcting when I was a child. But his methods created more pain and chaos than they alleviated. I understand that my father was doing what he knew how to do and what he thought was best to help get me in line. But as I grew older, the physical discipline only served to keep us estranged. I continued to act out and refused to allow him to control me.

My father always had his own ideas of what my life should look like. However, I never cared about those ideas. I just did what I knew that I needed to do to move forward. It remained a tremendous challenge to even live in the same house with the man. So my mother came up with the idea that I should move out. When I was about 22-years-old, I moved from my mother's home and into my grandmother's basement.

Initially the plan worked out wonderfully. Moving into my own place was a very happy and proud time for me. I felt that I finally had some independence and control over my life. I also had privacy, which allowed me to have my friends over without feeling embarrassed about being cursed out by my father or having him wobble home drunk. But what started out as a haven turned into my own personal hell. The truth of the matter was that even though I had escaped my father physically, I still brought all of my demons and insecurities and fears right along with me.

As time went on I started to behave like my father in certain ways. I began drinking for the first time in my life. At first it was just social drinking. Then I started getting drunk and picking fights with people. After a while I escalated to using drugs and hanging out with the wrong crowd. My new "friends" were disrespectful to my grandparents, as was I. The situation spiraled out of control very quickly. I tried to get a handle on things by going away to college. This was my first stint in college and I felt sure that the new environment would help me get control over the negative aspects of my life.

For a while things were better. But then my father died. The intensity of my grief was shocking to me, given the state of our relationship. I felt confused and had difficulty coming to terms with the fact that I truly loved and missed my father despite how he treated me. My fear of him and our inability to get along were the main things that I'd been aware of in our relationship. The belief that I could never please or satisfy him filled the available space in my mind—until he died. And then it was too late.

After he was dead suppressed feelings of love began to bubble to the surface. Unfortunately, the first coping mechanism that I turned to was alcohol, his drug of choice. Prior to that time my alcohol use had been more social. But after my father's death my drinking became heavier and heavier. I started smoking too. By the end of the semester following my father's death, I had graduated from drinking and smoking marijuana to smoking crack cocaine. I was very quickly spiraling out of control. That's when I moved back into my grandmother's basement. I thought that the familiar surroundings and the love of my grandmother would help me get a handle on my situation. But it didn't. Instead, that was when the hell truly began. My decline culminated in the ultimate disgrace many months later, when I had to be escorted out of my grandmother's basement by the police.

I was so afraid of facing my loss that I allowed my life to devolve into the chaos of drug addiction and, eventually, homelessness. Fear debilitated me, as it does to so many of us. Even if you've pushed your fear away and refuse to acknowledge that it's there, it will still run the choices that you make until you face it. Fear changes how you see the world around you and even yourself. Unchecked fear can be deadly.

Of course, there is healthy fear, which is designed to keep us safe. There are certain things and experiences that we are best steering clear of altogether. A healthy dose of fear can keep us from engaging things that can do us great harm. But unhealthy fear is based on delusions and misconceptions, emotional baggage or negative labels. Fear can also originate in the experience of not being able to fit in. All of those things combined to create the experience of intense fear in me.

Though we didn't have a good relationship, the truth was that I didn't know how to handle my father's loss. I developed a terrible fear of death to the point where I couldn't even turn the light out at night. If I did, I'd have to sleep with my Bible. If all else failed, I would drink until I passed out. Fear completely reshaped my life into something unrecognizable. It created a false image that I began to believe was the truth about me.

The image that fear creates can be so convincing that even you will stop questioning it. This image might be based on the belief that you're a loser or that you shouldn't have the things you desire, that you're undeserving. You might believe that you should just settle for mediocrity. You may believe that you don't have what it takes to have a life of meaning. But none of that is based in reality.

For me, my beliefs were based in large part on things that

my father had said to me over the years. I ended up living out those cruel words as if they were the gospel truth. But I was the one who took them on as an unconscious belief system and a self-concept. We create our own fears based on how we see the world and our place in it. There are many different aspects of fear that develop within us based on our experiences. For example, I developed a fear of death. But for some of the people it may be the fear of success or illness or being homeless and unable to take care of oneself. There can be fear surrounding the ability to follow through on realizing a dream or being accepted by others. Unfortunately we often manifest our fears because that's where we've placed our attention, so that's what shows up in our experience. We've made the mistake of focusing on what we don't want and speaking about our fears regularly and with great emotion.

What we're doing in these instances is telling God that we believe more in our fears than we do in grace, our gifts and our abilities. If we've experienced good fortune or success, we're saying that we believe in our fears even more than we believe in our history. The thought comes that says, *Oh, I don't know if I will ever be able to replicate what I did before so let me not even try.* If we fail in some areas, then our thoughts may say, *This must be the truth of who I am. I am a failure.* Not succeeding in something that was important to you is difficult. But it's not who you are as a person. It's just an experience.

When people have been hurt by failure, the pain can lead them to make excuses about why they can't do something in the future. Giving up feels easier than trying and possibly failing again. *Why should I try? Why should I apply myself? This isn't for me.* But the truth is that you're capable of achieving your goals, no matter how many times you have to try before you accomplish them. Moreover, you'll be able to handle the success that arises from those accomplishments.

Fear of success is insidious because, to most people, it feels counterintuitive to believe that they would ever shy away from claiming their hard earned victories. But feeling incapable of managing the spotlight and the responsibilities associated with your achievements can be just as debilitating as fear of failure. You don't need to know in advance how you will deal with abundance. You simply need to take the action steps necessary that will put you on the right path.

The alternative is to give up and allow negative beliefs to become self-fulfilling prophecies. I stopped reading as a young person because I believed it when others told me that I couldn't learn. I stopped attempting to understand math because someone said that I couldn't do it. I believed what teachers and so-called experts told me about myself. By the time I ended up in special education I believed wholeheartedly that I belonged there—and that I'd never be able to do better. Then, when I was told that I had ADD, I believed that, too.

Over the years, I set up an elaborate belief system to support the lies about who I was and what I was capable of. I was afraid to apply to colleges in high school because I didn't think I'd be able to write an essay or complete an application, though I desperately wanted to continue my education. I feared joining the debate team because I thought I'd be called a fool, since I'd been repeatedly told that I didn't speak well. For a time I stopped auditioning for musical solos because I had a fear of being lackluster. It was easier not to try.

Fear keeps us stuck in our small world. We think the larger world is for other people. It's like hearing an agnostic say, "God may work for you but God will not work for me." We say, *I believe success works for you but I don't believe success can work for me. So I'll just deal with mediocrity. I'll play small.* Few people consciously say this to themselves, but that's the end result no matter how we may dress it up. Sometimes this unspoken (or unconscious) agreement simply looks like being lazy. But it's not so much that the person is lazy as it is that they're petrified of not measuring up. They are afraid to answer the call on their lives because of the deep-seated belief that their effort will be in vain.

Being a perfectionist is also part of the fear factor. Perfectionists succumb to the idea, which says, *if I make a mistake I am not good enough. I am not the right one.* We learn to be afraid of mistakes because we're taught that only winning matters. Mistakes aren't a necessary part of the process. In fact, too many mistakes are an indicator that we'll never amount to anything substantial. Think about the questions that we ask our children. *What is your GPA? Are you an honor student? Did you win the game?* Well meaning though we may be, what we're doing is trying to quantify our children's potential and worthiness with numbers, scores and competitive rankings.

The truth is that none of those markers can scratch the surface of our children's innate potential in any way. But we've been taught (and therefore teach the next generation) that if you don't measure up you won't make the cut. You won't get the deal or the contract or the scholarship that will change your life. Someone else will get it and they'll be better, happier and more successful than you. These are all terrible, soul-destroying lies that keep us searching desperately for validation and fulfillment outside of ourselves.

Perfectionism is as debilitating as any other form of anxiety. I experienced this when I was singing. No matter how well I did it was never good enough. No matter how long I practiced, something would happen that would make my efforts invalid. Perfectionists have a very hard time celebrating the good. They only concentrate on the fact that their effort was *not as good as it could have been*. They never get to enjoy or relax in their contribution since they're always trying to measure up to an unrealistic rubric.

Fear has the potential to tear apart the fabric of our lives. But it's not something that will ever go away in our human experience. We must learn to live with healthy fear and distinguish it from unhealthy or overwhelming fear. We must change our thinking to help alleviate some of the unnecessary hardships and consequences related to it.

Most of the time fear resides in our minds. There's usually nothing physically happening in our environment that's a threat to our safety or wellbeing. When fear crops up, we can learn to recognize it for what it is: a lack of confidence and trust. We don't trust that the things that we want will ever be attained. We aren't confident that the things we don't want can be avoided or handled with courage and dignity should they actually arise. Facing fear means challenging those misconceptions by pushing through. It may feel like walking through the valley of the shadow of death, you must walk. If you keep walking you'll get to the other side.

The most powerful way to dispel fear is to talk about it. Choose a trusted friend to listen as you unburden your heart. Or open yourself to God in prayer. Self talk also works to expose the unrealistic nature of most of our fears. I have a prayer that I say when I'm working through fear. It's very simple and it goes like this: *God please remove all my fears guide me and direct me to what you would have me to see and what you would have me to do.* Immediately the anxiety shifts and I come into alignment with whatever I'm supposed to be working toward. The fear that made everything cloudy and uncertain is dispelled by clarity.

Make a practice of relying on God's power to sustain you. Seek ye first the kingdom of God… and all else shall be added unto you. Matthew 6:33(NKJV) The kingdom of God is within. So go inside and see what is there to be done. Allow yourself to be directed to a place of calm and clarity, which will propel you past the fear. This process is simple to say and understand, but not easy to do. It's not easy because we like to live in our heads. We also like to live in the past, in our mistakes and missteps. We've memorized stories shaped by our fear, which we tell ourselves (and others) any chance we get. But we must always remember that we have the power to tell ourselves a new story and live that out.

Other stories originate from the collective consciousness of our society. We hear so many depressing narratives on television or read them in the newspaper. These stories advance an agenda of fear without spending much time describing other, more life affirming aspects of our collective experience. They are meant to elicit suspicion and division in those of us who watch, read or hear them. But this doesn't represent the full truth. It's a perspective that is just one piece of a larger whole.

If your perspective isn't based in love, then it's not the truth. It's the point of view of some person, entity or collective with an agenda. I invite you to ask yourself who or what is trying to influence your opinion and what is their agenda? Buying into anyone else's ploy is a sure way to keep yourself blocked, stopped and silenced.

There are certain areas where, collectively speaking, human beings tend to experience large amounts of fear-based thinking. Love and money are just two of those areas. People seem to think that money is the most important form of wealth. But this isn't true. Money is just one form of abundance. When we push past our fears surrounding finances, we can get present to the fact that money is just currency. It's important because we must deal with it as part of our human experience. But at its core, money is a form of flowing energy: you either pull it towards you or push it away.

Contrary to everything that we've ever been taught, nobody owns money. Or should I say, no one owns the energetic flow of wealth and abundance, of which money is but a singular representation. When you die your will and money stays right here and end up in someone else's pocket. Money is for our temporary use and enjoyment and that is all. It is always available. But it's our fear surrounding the idea of lack and limitation that can stop us from experiencing money in this way. We have our hands balled up in fear and yet still expect money to be able to enter into a closed fist. It's not possible. We must be receptive. Fear blocks our receptivity to that which we need and desire most.

As we mentioned before, fear of success is another concern that's prevalent amongst people of all walks of life. People are successful when they realize that they're doing what they want to do in life. You get to set the bar for success. It won't look the same for you as it looks for this superstar or that NBA player. We start to experience fear in relation to success when we decide to take on society's measure of achievement rather than listening to our own hearts and minds. As we become less aware of our own internal definition we stop moving in the direction of that sacred purpose.

If you look to others for validation, you may fall into the

trap of people pleasing rather than pursuing your truth. But you can never experience fulfillment in this way, no matter how many material items you collect along the way. People pleasing is a fear-based activity; it's avoidance behavior mixed with the disbelief that your authentic identity isn't powerful or unique enough to find fulfillment. Put the habit of people pleasing to rest by focusing on yourself and staying in your own lane. Make a practice of challenging the thoughts, opinions and ideas that have taken up residence in your mind. How many of them actually belong to you? Only when you begin to separate the wheat from the chaff will you ultimately be able to let go of this destructive form of self-sabotage.

Fear will crop up at pivotal points of advancement to block the manifestation of your greatest desires. When that happens, take some deep breaths and do a quick meditation. Think about the end goal and visualize yourself achieving that goal. Visualization is a way of creating in your own mind the outcome that you want to experience. You don't have to know all the steps to get there but seeing and feeling the joy of making it happen allows your mind to accept the inevitability of the outcome.

I was given a vision months before I was shot in the head. It was a vision of me as a teacher and a speaker being received by grateful audiences. It was a vision of success. I had no idea how I was going to achieve what I saw in my imagination or that it would take so long or that I would have to go through such tremendous upheaval and trauma to get there. But I am here now. An internal transition had to take place in order to get me into alignment with the vision that was given to me.

Likewise, we all have transitions to make on our journey. There will come a time when you must give up your old ideas and conversations in order to accept a higher vision for the unfolding of your life. You must give up the idea of low self-worth. You must give up listening to the naysayers. You must stand in the conviction that if you can see it, you can achieve it. Visualize the goals that you want to achieve with the same dedication that you use for your meditation and prayer. You may want to take a few moments every morning, every evening and at certain points during the day to refresh your mind.

There's a twofold benefit to this process. First, it helps your vision become much clearer and more detailed. Secondly, it helps to alleviate any lingering fear as you place your focus on what you want, rather than all the things that could go wrong. The fear will naturally dissipate as you gain greater clarity and understanding regarding your next action steps.

Taking decisive action is critically important. You don't rest on the information that you've been given. You move quickly, knowing that if you must fine-tune your steps you'll be given the information and the know-how to make the adjustments. Taking action also helps you become clearer about the ways in which you may have stopped yourself by believing in your fears rather than challenging them.

The next step is to make sure that you name your fear. This part of the process can be very tricky. Oftentimes, we think we're afraid of one thing, but deep down our fears have a much deeper meaning. For example, you may think that you're afraid that your boyfriend is going to leave you. But what you're really afraid of is being alone. You may not even love your boyfriend. Yet you'll fight to hold onto him, not realizing that you are actually terrified of abandonment, a source of anxiety that goes far beyond your current love life.

We must get clarity about the underlying fears that may be operating within us, which are much more powerful because they are unconscious. This is where we take our journals out and write. We write and write until there's nothing left. Start off at the top of your page by writing, "I am afraid of..." Then fill in the blank. Write what you believe will happen as a result of experiencing whatever it is that you dread. In other words, do a fear inventory. One way to do this exercise is to write, "I am fearful because of this... If this happens then that will happen..." Keep going deeper and deeper, as far down as you need to go to get to the root of your fears.

Sometimes our deepest fears involve the idea of not being enough. Fear of being unworthy plagues so many of us in Western society because we're actively taught that we aren't good enough. It's a message that is ingrained in us as part of our cultural norms. We must buy certain products, have a certain job or look a certain way before we can be deemed worthy by society's standards. Moreover, many of us have experienced some form of bias based on who we are—be it homophobia, racism or sexism—that operates in addition to the traditional cultural messages. All of these factors combine to create the messages, which say, *I can't... I shouldn't... I won't be able to.*

These ideas are based on pervasive social dynamics that are put in effect to hold people in their respective places. It could be classism or ageism or ableism. Anything that shows up to limit you—no matter what it is—is not the truth. The truth is that you are a perfectly whole, capable, intelligent and extraordinary individual who can do whatever you set your mind to. You can become whatever you want to become. The truth is that you are the creation of the Almighty God, who has intentionally called all of us to this time in history for a particular purpose. We were all born for something. Fear wants to stop us from recognizing this fact. Our job is to push through, to realize what we've come to the planet to do and get busy doing it.

Reflections

I related to...

_____

_____

_____

_____

_____

_____

_____

_____

_____

_____

_____

_____

_____

_____

CHAPTER SEVEN

Some Other to Win: Allowing
your victories to push you toward
achieving your next big goal

There is a hymn, which says, "Yield not to temptation for yielding is sin; each victory will help you some other to win..." My spiritual mother, a woman named Ruby Burruss, always reminded me of this hymn whenever I came to tell her about having achieved success in some endeavor. She would look at me with pride in her eyes and say, "some other to win." She was encouraging me to reach for another victory, a bigger goal. I call Mother Burruss my spiritual mother because she was the wife of the pastor of my childhood church, Zion, in Anderson South Carolina. The Bishop and Mother Burruss lived in Atlanta GA; however as General Overseer and First Lady they served 32 churches comprising the National Convention of the Churches of God Holiness USA.

Mother Burruss had a beautiful singing voice. So she really enjoyed hearing me sing and encouraged my musical talents. But she also admonished me to stay in school and work hard to excel in my studies. The more I listened to her, the more she took the time to speak with me. Mother Burruss saw the good in me when so many others didn't. She was an inspiration throughout my life. Before she died, she said to me, "Brother Dale, you have the love of God in you because I put it in you." And she was right.

Mother Burruss was, for me, a human manifestation of the unconditional love of God. She was a trusted guide and mentor, always reminding me to surround myself with good friends who cared about me. She even gave me advice about girls. Mother Burruss had a way of telling me which girls were worth my time and effort. She would also give me advice in boys. Having such a watchful eye she would often say to me "leave them boys alone, they don't mean you any good." Her advice was almost never wrong. She had a gift of seeing into human nature and finding the good in others, especially me.

My relationship with Mother Burruss was so different than the relationships with my parents at home. She listened to me and gave me instruction and correction in a way that I could hear. Her words and actions never diminished me by talking loud or hitting me or calling me out of my name. Instead she encouraged me and always with a smile. At one point there was an annual church convention happening in Atlanta. Mother Burruss allowed me to live with her and the Bishop so that I could attend the convention. The experience was incredible. It was so new to me to be around such positivity and unconditional love. I just flourished in that environment.

It was very important to Mother Burruss that I learned what the Scriptures said about growing into a respectful young man of integrity. She called it becoming a holy brother. I did my best to listen to everything she said and when I didn't listen, she would gently remind me, "You can fool me, Brother Dale, but you can't fool God. God knows everything." This woman took the time to plant seeds in my life without expectation of immediate gratification. She just continued to love me unconditionally. She literally raised me. My own mother pulled back and allowed Mother Burruss to counsel me because she could see how much I was getting out of the relationship.

Of all the lessons Mother Burruss taught me, one of the most powerful was the lesson about goal setting—some other to win. From her I learned how to change my station in life by keeping myself focused. "Some other to win" meant that whenever I accomplished something of any significance that I was to go to the next level. I was to put my attention on moving to the next step rather than rest on my laurels.

The power in this work is to set a new goal that requires you to keep growing, to push yourself beyond your limits. We've all heard about the benefits of goal setting in every self-help book and business advice column on the market. It's deeply ingrained in our collective consciousness. We know that we must set goals in order to be productive. But oftentimes we don't practice this critical skill successfully. We get stopped for variety of reasons. Some people are just lazy and not motivated to set goals in the first place. They don't want to do the footwork or labor over the process rigorously to get the results.

Sometimes we stop because of fear, as we discussed. We may feel a lack of confidence that we have the ability to actually attain our goals. Some of the fear may be based on what we were told as children about our skills and abilities (or lack thereof). Until we dispel those ideas they remain inside us, unconscious but active. And if we've internalized those beliefs we can be stopped by what amounts to someone else's fear and insecurity. They didn't achieve what they wanted in life, so they've told you that you can't do it either. Now you live out someone else's pathology and will continue to do so until you decide to say no more.

It takes an incredibly courageous person to push past such treacherous stumbling blocks and say, *not me! I'm better than that! I might not do it the way the next person does it, but I'm going to put forth my best effort.* And sometimes that's all it takes: put forth your best effort and persevere.

Sometimes the problem lies in the fact that people set the wrong goals. And by "wrong" I mean they're not trying to achieve what they truly want. Instead, they're trying to reach goals that someone else has determined for them. "Someone else" may be society or parents or friends or teachers. A person may not have any idea what he or she really desires because their dreams have been sublimated by the opinions and needs of others. Even if you do achieve these externally motivated goals, the success will lack a feeling of real accomplishment and fulfillment because deep down in your heart, you don't really even want it! It's not your goal. It's not part of the call that's been placed on your life.

You have to be assertive enough to give those people back their dreams. Then rekindle the flame of your own desires. Put your time and effort where they belong. This is usually easier said than done. We never want to disappoint those we love the most. But when we respect each other's personalities—as well as their talents and gifts—we open up a space to allow the people we love to bring forth their gifts in their own way. That's how we help them to become even better people. In that environment success, joy, creativity and fulfillment are assured. We all become better people.

But if we don't have the courage to conquer our own goals, we may never feel the joy that comes from living our purpose. We may feel relief, or pleasure at being competent and rewarded for our skills. But joy will remain illusive because it comes from tapping into our authentic desires. So be aware of setting the right goals. And make sure that your goals don't simply take you down the path of least resistance. Setting goals that don't challenge you is simply another way of taking the easy way out, regardless of whether the "easy way" is in alignment with righteousness.

Ask yourself: are your goals in alignment with your passion? Or are they in alignment with what you *think* you can do well enough to become a good provider? Being able to provide for yourself and others (if you choose to have a family) is extremely important. But always remember that you can find ways to provide a good lifestyle for yourself while persistently reaching to achieve greatness in whatever field you consider to be your passion.

When I was younger my pastor couldn't understand why I didn't want to be a pastor like him. Instead, I felt called to minister to the marginalized, the disenfranchised and dispossessed—the least among us. I was passionate about that culture. I didn't feel the same yearning to lead a congregation. My desire was to help those who needed me in the church without walls that resided in the world outside our door.

We must stand firm in our beliefs, which will allow us to go for the goals that are in alignment with our spirit and our intentions. As we talked about before, each of us has a very specific calling on our lives. We will never be fully at rest, or fully alive and invigorated, until we answer that call.

Ask yourself why you want to achieve the goal that you are working toward? Why do you want that degree? Why do you want this job you've applied for? Who wants you to have the job? Is the desire from your heart or from your peers and family? What is the payoff for your achievements? If the benefit of accomplishing a goal is just to get paid or to gain prestige, you might want to rethink that goal. There will always be ways to experience abundance and success while still honoring the call of God. Money isn't everything. Our spirits thrive when we move with the flow, agreeing to take the action steps that are placed before us toward an objective that is bigger than ourselves.

There will still be those occasions where we run into obstacles that feel insurmountable. This is when, as my godmother always told me, we look to the hills from which cometh our help. According to the 121 Psalm "our help cometh from the Lord, the Lord which made the heavens and the earth." (NKJV) The help that you need to continue in these moments of trouble lies in the hands of God; it's inside you because God is inside you. Look beyond your mind, your thoughts, your ego and your ability to "make things happen" to that which is eternal. It is here that we enter a prayerful mode. We humbly and trustingly look to the hills because that is where we'll find the solution to whatever has blocked our path.

To this day, when something isn't working for me or things have the appearance of being stopped, I go to the hills in my mind. I go to God. People think that you're weak if you're seeking help beyond your own power and resources. The world will tell you that you're inadequate if you can't handle everything on your own. But that's wrong. When you surrender to the power of Spirit, you are at your greatest strength because God is able to speak through you. There's a channel to the divine that opens up when we go to the hills. There is clarity, understanding, hope, trust, peace and patience waiting to be revealed when we go to the hills.

All of these qualities of the Spirit are necessary when we talk about progressing through life. But it's crucial to cultivate patience, which can mean the difference between persevering and giving up. When you start thinking that what you're working toward is never going to happen, that's the ego leading you down a stray path. The voice of God says hold your course. When we set goals that don't seem to come to fruition quickly enough, it's easy to feel like a failure. But trust that your goals are unfolding in perfect timing. God's time is not necessarily your time. If you don't develop the patience to discern the season of waiting from the season of action, then giving up will become inevitable.

Lack of patience is a huge reason why people fail to see their dreams take shape. We fear that if things aren't working right now, it means they will never work. Then we wash our hands of the effort. But that is anxiety and impatience speaking. We're taught to be anxious prematurely and for nothing. When you feel anxiety take hold in your mind, make a practice of stopping to examine the thoughts and asking, *are these thoughts true? Can I release this anxiety and work on patience right now? Where is this anxiety coming from? Can I address the root cause, rather than take rash action that may pull me away from my goals?*

Anxiety causes us to doubt our abilities, make ourselves wrong or become desperate, thereby knocking us off track. By addressing the anxiety and allowing it to dissipate we keep ourselves steadily moving ahead. We're no longer deceived by the appearance of negative circumstances. We may also realize that we need to tweak either our objectives or our approach to manifesting our goals. We may not be in alignment with the fullness of the vision that's being created within.

That's why it's so important to look to the hills. If you're struggling in a marriage or any kind of relationship, look to the hills. When you're dealing with your kids, look to the hills. If you've got an addiction problem, look to the hills. If you've got an employment problem, look to the hills because that's where your help is coming from. Ideas, insights and the faith to do the impossible come forth when you look to the hills for guidance. To the world it may look like you're doing something daring or impossible because you're reaching for your highest aspirations. But you're in the safest place that you can be because you're resting in God. When you rest in God, you rest in right action, right thinking and right motives. You can't go wrong there. The answers will come and the way will be made.

This faith gives us the persistence to keep moving forward and to do so with a joyful heart. When we walk with faith and joy, we become immune to the urge to complain about our circumstances. Mother Burruss always cautioned me to never complain. Complaining drains your spirit and your mind of its will to keep going. It provides you with excuses to settle for lack and limitation in your life, while you whine about not having more. It allows you to admit defeat prematurely. Complaint creates stagnant energy and there's no possibility for transformation in it.

We complain when we don't see the gift that we've been given in a situation. And make no mistake—there's a gift in any situation, no matter how terrible it may seem. There's a quality or an insight or a strength waiting to be born from our sorrow, if we can manage to catch sight of it. One of my professors at Emory always told us, "Shun not the struggle because it's a gift from God." In order to get to your purpose you must engage in the struggle. The next step on your journey will arise from the insights that you find there.

Of course, we must remember that there's a big difference between having a testimony borne from struggle and having a story. When you complain you get stuck in your story. I honestly believe that there is always a reason for everything that happens to us. There's a reason you had that terrible automobile accident and are now wheelchair-bound. There's a reason that your husband or wife left you. There's a reason that you got fired from your job. And it's not a reason that requires you to blame yourself or feel terrible or engage in complaint about how the world did you wrong.

The real reason has everything to do with your growth, edification, transformation and purpose. The reason has to do with us coming to the understanding that we are unlimited beings. We may seem limited if we look at ourselves with the lens of our five senses, which is what most people do. But we are eternal spiritual beings. No matter what has transpired, we are more powerful now than we ever were before. We're still growing and changing, making the choice to move through the struggle with grace rather than complaint.

When I was shot in the head my way of being change dramatically. But I have no remorse or regret about the incident because I believe that I'm fully in alignment with God's plan for my life. I don't think what happened was "evil," despite whatever personal intentions my attackers may have had. I understand that I am part of a much larger plan. We each get to decide how to interpret the events that unfold in our lives. No matter what others may say or how they may perceive us, the deciding factor is how we perceive ourselves. That determines our ability to stand tall no matter what.

When you complain you're telling the universe that there's something wrong. There was a mistake made somewhere and something bad happened as a result. Ultimately, you're making sure that you stay in your sadness and dysfunction rather than rising above it and moving into a position of empowerment. You are agreeing to stay in victimhood. But you're not a victim. When you change your story you change your perception of yourself within that story. This isn't an easy process. But we must move through the difficulties of life in order to reach the place where we claim our transformation. Otherwise we remain incomplete.

This is what it means when the apostle Paul says in Romans 12:2b, "But be ye transformed by the renewing of your mind." (NKJV) When faced with hardships, it is our minds that must transform before we can see the change in the outer circumstance. Being shot in the head offered me a tremendous gift in that it was the catalyst for me to stop living a backwards life. I was finally able to give up the behaviors that had dogged me for so many years and that seemed like I would never be able to release. By choosing to see a horrible situation for the lessons and the good that it held, I was able to propel myself from a place of deep despair to where I am now. I never could have done that by wallowing in sadness and complaint.

Let go of your story, which is based on limited perception and fear, not truth. Within our stories there may be elements that we want to hide, things that make us feel ashamed. This is because we haven't embraced all parts of who we are and what we've been through and brought it all up to the light. It was very hard for me to tell the whole story about what led up to me being shot. I held shame and judgment about the part I played for a very long time. But as long as I hid from the truth I could never be healed. Once I let go of the shame I began to see that the circumstance was a way for God to intervene on my behalf. Intervention from a higher power invites us to come up out of darkness and into the light. For most people the intervention won't be as dramatic as what happened to me. Quite often the intervention is something good that you've been waiting on that finally comes to pass. All you have to do is step into receiving what's rightfully yours.

Sometimes we don't know how to get to the light because we've been in darkness so long. Darkness provides a comfort zone where people play small and feel that nothing is significant about them. But when you're called out you will see a whole new individual with a whole new purpose and plan for life. The 23rd Psalm v5 says that the table will be prepared before us. And that is exactly what happens as we move through life's difficulties: the table is being prepared for us that we may sit and feast from greater understanding, insight and joy, which is seeking expression through us.

When that happens, then not only are all of your needs met, but your cup truly runs over. Lives will be transformed because of who you are. Keep walking though the valley knowing that Goodness and mercy follows you and will continue following you all the days of your life. Just start where you are in this process. Like God told Moses when he was called to free the children of Israel out of bondage, use what is in your hand. Then you can build on what you have.

If you haven't been successful by the world's standards it can feel as though everyone else has moved ahead while you're still at life's starting gate, trying to figure out a way to break free. The ego stays busy worrying, complaining and comparing what you supposedly don't have to what other people supposedly do have. *Why am I not further ahead in life? What's wrong with me?* These thoughts are the ego trying to get you to stay stuck in your story. But we must never compare, never looked to others to confirm or deny our greatness and purpose.

Start where you are with gratitude. If you're far from achieving your goal, be grateful that you've been given a concept. Cultivate the concept with joyful expectation and patience. It takes time, perseverance and focus to allow the "little" to become "much" in our lives. You have to do your part. Use the wisdom that others have provided you to build on these techniques. Then you stick and stay.

Stick and stay is an old saying that I used hear in NA meetings after I became clean, meaning stick with your goal and do not be moved. People in recovery say this as shorthand for the agreement that no matter what happens, they'll maintain their sobriety at all costs. You are declaring *I will stay the course!* But this is a great truth for us all. Stick with your goals and the tide ultimately will turn in your favor. Make the commitment to not lose focus. Never give up the attention on your intention. If you get off track, regroup immediately. Don't pause or put it off. There's no reason. Believe in yourself and believe in the process, then see it through no matter what.

Reflections

I related to...

CHAPTER EIGHT

Not Here to Get, But Here to Let:
Helping others through giving

Life is full of choice points. We are all faced with circumstances, which give us the opportunity to love or to withhold, to show empathy or judgment, to give willingly or to hoard what we have. As children, we're taught that sharing and giving are good things and that we shouldn't hesitate to offer assistance to others. But as adults, our society often sends the exact opposite message. We're told, subtly or overtly, to keep what we have for ourselves. We're warned that if we give too much or too freely, we'll be taken advantage of by unscrupulous people.

There's a certain line of thinking that looks at a given situation and asks, *"What's in it for me? What can I get out of this deal?"* When we're ensnared by these kinds of thoughts we always want to know what angle will benefit us the most before making any kind of decision. Not only do we want to make sure that we're getting something in return for our investment of time or energy, but many of us even want something for nothing! But this is backwards thinking. And it actually prevents unhindered abundance from flowing into our lives.

Ask yourself: Am I primarily focused on giving or taking? Takers usually want the most benefits for the least effort. But when your primary energy is one of generosity, you seek to serve in ways that will benefit others as well as yourself. As a result, you're enlivened by your ability to connect with and serve others. You experience joy, peace and gratitude because you realize that your efforts have made things better for someone else.

Givers understand about the law of reciprocity. Giving and receiving are of equal importance. We can't give to the point that we're depleted of time, energy or abundance. Life requires us to receive in order to maintain our own health and wellbeing. Yet somehow human beings have, by and large, gotten out of balance. Some of us give so much that we deplete all of our resources; it becomes difficult to sustain ourselves, much less anyone else. Moreover, we don't know how to receive from others, even during those times when we may be desperately in need.

On the other end of the spectrum, there are people who think of themselves first, last and always. They refuse to help others even when they have the means and could easily do so. It can be very difficult for these people to see things from someone else's point of view. It's hard to determine how we, as a society, have gotten so out of balance. We've forgotten how to give to others with ease, grace and an open heart. We have trouble trusting that we'll receive everything we need to thrive without having to fight and scratch for it.

The truth is that we're part of the universal flow. But when we think only about our personal survival, we get out of touch with that flow. This is an immature way of thinking. Small children go through a *me-me-me* stage, where they're concerned primarily with getting their way and having their immediate desires fulfilled. This is a perfectly necessary and appropriate stage of development because children are just learning about the concept of "self" in relation to others. The problem comes when adults fall victim to this kind of childish behavior, which is based in fear and self-centeredness.

We can see this imbalance in various aspects of our modern life. When people scheme or cheat to get more than what they deserve they are living as people who lack consciousness (no matter how much money they may have in the bank). It's a "survival of the fittest" mentality. Self-preservation blocks us from seeing our part in creating a world of imbalance. People think they have to struggle to get what's coming to them, rather than letting their good flow freely to them. The art of allowing, of letting abundance flow, leaves ample space for others to receive their fair and equal share.

The focus on materialism in society has all but eclipsed the spiritual basis for expressing generosity. Instead, far too many of us live with chronic worry and fear, specifically the fear of not having enough of what we need to survive. But here's the trick: when you live as those who lack consciousness it doesn't matter how much you have. Your fear of not having enough will cause you to stay stuck in energetic and spiritual poverty—even if your bank account is bursting with money!

It can be very challenging to step back from our worldly viewpoint and see through the eyes of this spiritual principle, which says that there's more than enough to go around. We all have everything we need to not only survive, but to thrive. And it's our job to share that abundance whenever and wherever we can, to let it flow as a blessing to those around us.

Everyone has a part to play in the building of our collective experience here on the planet. There's no shortage of wealth or food or shelter or love or any of the things that human beings need to live happy and productive lives. The only thing that we need to change to experience this abundance is our mindset, our belief systems. We are here to "dwell in the land and feed on His faithfulness." Psalms 37:3b (NKJV) Contrary to what our society tells us, we are not here to claim the land. None of it belongs to us and it never will. But we are here to make it better, to bring beauty and increase where there is lack, to create peace and prosperity where there is deprivation.

The question is: what can I bring to my society? What can I bring to any situation I find myself in? How can I enhance my family and community? Asking questions like *what can I get out of this* serves no one. When you're willing to give of your time, attention and energy it does more than change the trajectory of your own life. It allows you to be the impetus for abundance and self-discovery to enter into someone else's life as well.

When I was a young man, I had a mentor who was the epitome of giving and kindness. This man changed my life forever. At the time, I was about 26-years-old, homeless and struggling to get off drugs. I had just been kicked out of yet another treatment center in South Carolina because I relapsed and began using crack cocaine again. By this time my father was deceased and I had been kicked out of my grandparents' basement. I'd just gotten out of the four-month jail stint and had nowhere to go. A friend of mine suggested that I come to Georgia with him to work a handyman job. That was how I found myself back in Atlanta doing plumbing work and trying to scrape by with enough to eat and hopefully a place to sleep at night.

One day while I was on the job, an older gentleman named Mr. Hollins came up and started talking to me. He asked me what my story was and I began to tell him about losing my father and getting hooked on drugs. I had flunked out of school and was in Atlanta really hoping to be able to get my life back together. I dreamed of going back to college and finally graduating, which didn't even seem possible at that time. That night, Mr. Hollins invited me to dinner. He told me, "Well, you know Mark you can spend the night with us."

The next morning he came and told me that he'd spoken with his wife and they both decided that they would like me to come and live with them. I desperately needed a place to stay and I couldn't believe that these people would open their home to me, a stranger, out of the goodness of their hearts. They had decided to take a leap of faith and invite me into their family. Mr. Hollins let me know that I would have certain responsibilities if I wanted to stay in their home. My job would be to keep the house clean. That sounded more than fair to me and I gratefully accepted.

Mr. and Mrs. Hollins were little bit older than my parents. They had a beautiful home and five grown, professional children. Their home was filled with love and positivity. It was a place where they lived their spiritual beliefs on a daily basis. They were prayerful people who focused on giving to others. When Mr. Hollins said that I could stay with them it meant the world to me. Here I was surrounded by these intelligent and successful individuals who also thought I was worthwhile. They were concerned about my wellbeing. They encouraged me and assured me that they were there to help and they were always true to their word.

Mr. Hollins taught me that a man should be able to take care of himself and pay his own way in the world. So it was very important that I be able to handle my chores, because that was my way of contributing to the household. He would even pay me for doing certain jobs outside of the work that we agreed that I would do. Mr. Hollins was the first man to teach me how to pay my own way in the world. I hadn't learned that lesson prior to meeting him even though I was an adult, a grown man in my 20s.

I'd come from a background where the men in my life spoke negativity into me and the other children. I had grown up believing that I was a deadbeat, a beggar and a bum and nothing that I did would be worthwhile. Here was a man who wasn't even related to me who was dissolving the negative energy around me by speaking spiritual truths over my life. He generously gave of his time, energy and wisdom to help me learn what I was capable of achieving. By telling me that a man should pay his own way and giving me the means to do so, Mr. Hollins was saying that I could be a man of integrity and respect. I could make my own way in the world. Through his belief I began to dissolve that false identity that had been built up in me since childhood.

Mr. Hollins made me a part of his family. They never treated me as though I was an outsider. I was invited to the dinner table like every other member of the family. When they went away to their cabin on the weekends, I was invited to go along. When they went to football games there was always a ticket for me as well. The members of that family gave to me in so many ways that I couldn't begin to list them all. But the things that made the most lasting impression on me were the love, encouragement and their belief that I could be more. What they gave was much more than any material possession could match: they gave me direction. They gave me a feeling of substance and hope.

When Mr. Hollins found out that I'd gone to Morehouse, he began to announce me as, "Marcus, the great Morehouse man. Marcus Aurelius, last of the great Roman Caesars!" He always saw greatness in me, even though I had come to them homeless and addicted to drugs. He would pray over me and affirm that I was going to finish my degree at Morehouse and that I would excel and do well in life.

Mr. Hollins shared his spiritual and intellectual wisdom with me, but he also instructed me in practical things that would help me to become self-sufficient. Prior to that time, no one had ever shown me how to take care of myself. Being that I'd been the youngest in my family, the adults and older children pretty much did everything for me. I never learned to stand on my own two feet. Around my father and the other men in my family, I pretty much disappeared. Around Mr. Hollins, on the other hand, I grew exponentially.

The Hollins family stuck with me through many ups and downs with me. At one point, after I'd lived with them for more than a year, my behavior forced Mr. Hollins to ask me to leave the family home. I had relapsed back into drugs. I'd been through my third treatment center by then and I still hadn't been able to stay clean. I stole money from one of his sons and then stole more money from his Christmas savings fund to feed my drug habit. I felt so bad about it that I told Mr. Hollins' son—and he let me have it! Then he did the thing that I was dreading: he said that we would have to tell his father.

When I admitted that I'd stolen money, Mr. Hollins said, "Marcus, I hate to do it but you're going to have to taste the elements." He put me out, and in my heart I knew that I deserved it. But Mr. Hollins still wasn't ready to give up on me. So in spite of everything that had happened, he still allowed me to sleep in his van. His only rule was that I obey his curfew and be in by 2 AM. But I'd stumble in at 4:00 or 5:00 some mornings. Sometimes I didn't come back at all. Mr. Hollins said, "Marcus, if you're not going to come home you must at least give us a call. Mildred and I worry about you, son, and we need to at least make sure that you're safe." I still wasn't able to do even that much.

My behavior forced him to make a difficult choice. Mr. Hollins put me out one final time and it was months before he would allow me to come back. I endured so much during that time on the street, including a trash can. Finally, I couldn't take it anymore and I knew that I needed to turn my life around. When I came back, truly repentant and ready to make amends, Mr. Hollins welcomed me back into the fold.

He was determined to keep showing me a different path until I found the strength and the courage to take it. There's an old saying, "You can lead a horse to water but you can't make him drink." Mr. Hollins would always say, "That's shit! You *can* make him drink. You just hold his head down there long enough and he'll drink!" That's what he tried to demonstrate with me. He held my head down until I drank. And I did. That's when I finally got sober and he was thrilled.

Mr. Hollins was the mentor that pulled me up when I was at my lowest. Through all the years that I struggled, their faith in me kept me believing in myself. Ultimately, I was able to reward their faith by turning my life around. Unfortunately, Mr. Hollins passed away just before he received the tickets in the mail for my Morehouse graduation ceremony. But his wife and children came to my graduation. It meant the world to me for them to see me accomplish something so monumental in my life.

Mr. Hollins' spiritual cup was so full that he could give and give and give—as he did with me—without depleting himself or his family's resources. He was surrounded by abundance on every front. He had more food than I had ever seen before. The family took more trips than anyone I had ever known. He had money and resources and friends and great respect in his community. He truly gave from the overflow. Mr. Hollins had retired from two occupations and his hard work had given him the wherewithal to live this kind of lifestyle with his family. But he didn't keep all that good fortune to himself. He shared generously whenever he could, and especially with me. He nourished me back to health.

I believe that Mr. Hollins' cup overflowed so greatly because he was a man of God. He truly believed that prayer changes things and he lived by example. And in being a giver, Mr. Hollins was demonstrating for me how to be a giver myself. I'd had the experience of being a taker. Those who are plagued by substance abuse behave selfishly and are always trying to get whatever they can to feed their habit. I'd taken from my parents, my grandparents, my friends and other family members and never thought twice about it. I didn't understand the concept of being able to generate and provide for others. Mr. Hollins taught me how to be a productive and responsible member of society. In short, he taught me how to be a man.

Mr. Hollins was a living example of the phrase, "You can't out give God." When we want to embody that type of spiritual light and be a magnet for abundance, we must start by giving of what they already have. There is no other way. You can't behave selfishly and expect to get more from the universe. The commitment to giving and serving others is what puts you on the path to abundance.

When there's need or lack in your life, do your inventory. First ask yourself, *in what areas am I lacking?* Then ask, *what will it take for me to get to the place where the need is fulfilled? Am I willing to take responsibility for doing and saying whatever is necessary to fulfill the need that I've uncovered?* This was one of the greatest lessons that Mr. Hollins taught me: to be responsible for me and my actions. Passing the buck, blaming others or making others responsible for my behavior is the epitome of irresponsibility and a lack of consciousness. It's an energy based in scarcity and fear.

It's impossible for lasting abundance to manifest when you're blocked in this way. In my case, I wasn't putting forth the effort to have my life work. I had to participate in my own growth and healing. I had to stay committed with my follow-through on a consistent basis in order to attract more abundance into my world. Commitment and participation are integral to experiencing genuine reciprocity. We cannot live abundantly without the energy of reciprocity being active in our lives. In other words, we must give in order to receive. That's just the way life works.

Participating in the giving and receiving process lets the universe know that you understand that you have more than enough to share, no matter where you are in your life in this given moment. When I first showed up on Mr. Holland's doorstep I had absolutely nothing. I started participating by literally sweeping the kitchen floor. That was all I could do back then. But I did it with a heart filled with gratitude for having been given the opportunity to provide that service for that beautiful family.

Mrs. Hollins never wore shoes around the house. But when she walked through that kitchen, the floor was so spotless she never had to worry about the bottoms of her feet getting dirty. She was so impressed with the dedication that I showed in my cleaning jobs that she told her husband. Mr. Hollins came back to me and said, "Mildred really likes how you swept that floor and cleaned up her kitchen."

It meant a great deal to me that my hard work was acknowledged and appreciated. And I said to myself, *if that's what there is for me to do then I'm going to keep cleaning up her kitchen and do it right! I'm going to make sure that she's knows how much I appreciate her kindness.* I put my heart into that humble job of sweeping their kitchen floor. Committing to my chores was the best I could give back then and it was enough. Recognize that no matter where you are in life you have the opportunity to participate in giving and making life better for someone else.

We must never take for granted those who choose to share their wealth and their love with us. No one is obligated to give you anything in this world. We must never forget that and remain thankful for the blessings that we receive. Gratitude multiplies things to be grateful for. In other words, the more you are grateful for, the more you will have. The more you have, the more you can give.

We can use our resources to improve the lives of others in big and small ways. Our giving doesn't always have to be about giving money. In fact, sometimes money is the least of it. Mr. Hollins and his family were a prime example of the idea that sometimes it's more about the love and commitment that we show to each other. Of course, it's always wonderful to share financial abundance as well. This can be a touchy subject for people because of the belief in scarcity surrounding finances that many of us have been taught. There's no getting around it though: part of this equation does have to do with sharing money and whatever financial abundance you have. Tithing, giving to charities, supporting friends and loved ones—all of these are crucial to the development of wealth consciousness. What you give away, you get more of. So those who are generous with their time and money tend to have more time and money flowing into their lives.

It doesn't matter how much you give. What matters is that you give something. Everything doesn't have a price tag. And when something does have a price tag think carefully about whether or not you can pay it. If you can pay, then do it with a glad heart. If you can't give financially, then move on with a clear conscience. You may not be able to give money to a worthy person or cause, but perhaps you can share your wisdom, expertise, time, skills or connections. Whatever you have to give is valuable.

We can all build win-win situations for ourselves and others when we choose to look through the lens of prosperity. When you give consciously and consistently it helps you to change your mindset about your own ability to generate wealth. You begin to see yourself as someone who has more than enough, even if you've never seen yourself that way before. You see yourself as a giver rather than a taker. You get to see how your own cup runneth over.

When you're connected to the Source you recognize there's no need to hold on to the little bit that you have. More will always be given. Have you ever heard people complain that they can't help others because they are living on a fixed income? I know I have. Or they complain that they're living from paycheck to paycheck. They have a set amount of money coming in, so they can't possibly give anything extra. If you're one of those people, I invite you to ask yourself: who fixed the income? If you go straight to the Source, you realize that what was fixed at one amount can just as easily be fixed at a higher amount.

In 1 Corinthians 2:9, we are told, "Eyes have not seen nor ears heard, nor have entered into the heart of man the things which God has prepared for those who love Him." (NKJV) We just have to trust Him and believe that we can receive. Look to see the demonstration of faith in your life. Rely upon the Masters teachings as recorded in Luke 6:38, "Give and ye shall receive: good measure, pressed down, shaken together, and running over will be put into your bosom…" (NKJV) It's just that simple. But you have to let go of the fear and the attachment to the belief that life is all about getting. It's really not. Having a wonderful and abundant life is all about letting and allowing the goodness of God to flow through us.

I'm forever grateful for meeting a man like Mr. Hollins and the rest of his family. I know that God put him in my path to help me redirect and transform my entire life by teaching me about the power of giving. When we are able to give at that level, there's no telling how many people will be affected by our generosity and our willingness to step out and be the hands of God operating here on Earth. Because God works through us as we help, uplift and support each other on this incredible journey.

Reflections

I related to...

_____

_____

_____

_____

_____

_____

_____

_____

_____

_____

_____

_____

_____

CHAPTER NINE

Drop the Material, See the Spiritual:
"Walking the bridge from reason to faith"

In Western society people tend to see reason—the capacity to apply logic to our experiences, to quantify perspective by turning it into verifiable fact—as the ultimate state of being. I think therefore I am. We believe that being intelligent or clever is what makes a person a worthwhile individual. A high functioning, well-reasoned mind is the best weapon to have in the battle to meet life's challenges and overcome obstacles. So we seek out advanced degrees. We go after positions of power where we can make more money. And we rely on the belief that our chances of attaining these goals are directly related to the prowess of our intellect. We want to be the smartest guy in the room because that designation means we're valuable and our lives have meaning.

But reason can only take you so far. It is limited. You can live from the mind, but the mind is not all that there is. Even the most brilliant thinkers can only grasp so much from a purely intellectual standpoint. However, as spiritual entities we are limitless and our possibilities are endless. We shortchange ourselves when we stick with the limited beliefs that say that the intellect is the only vehicle for success or self- development. We struggle trying to make things happen on our own power and are left wondering why we get stuck.

The truth is that we can't see the big picture because we're trapped inside the frame. Once you get outside of that frame it becomes possible to witness a clearer depiction of the world. Only faith—our willingness to connect with and rely on Spirit—can bring us to this expanded viewpoint. Faith moves us into the extraordinary position of being able to see more than what our senses can tell us. But we must make the conscious choice to cross the bridge from reason to faith.

The metaphor of "crossing the bridge" is one that I learned in my 12-step program. It implies that we're going on a journey, leaving the shore of our known world of addiction and venturing into the unknown life that awaits as we take hold of our sobriety. This journey will require us to give up the "I know" syndrome, which is the idea that all that there is lies within the scope of our knowledge. The fastest way to shut down real transformation is to hear a new idea and say, "Oh, I already know that."

For example, people will say, "I know all about finances and savings" but they're broke. Or they will say, "I know all about what it takes to make it through school," but they've never attained their college degree. They say, "I know what drugs and alcohol do to you," but they still can't stay clean. First of all, if you already know something that's of great spiritual or philosophical value, you'll be able to demonstrate the efficacy of that insight. In other words, when you embody what you "know" you'll be able to live the principles and manifest the results that you wish to see take shape.

Anything less is the ego trying to circumvent the process of growth and development. The ego will tell you, "You don't have to take that difficult journey because you already know what's waiting for you on the other side." But we can't just skip to the end. We must get present to the reasons why it frightens us to give up the idea of knowing. We must get comfortable with the idea that there's so much that we have yet to understand. Life may be asking us to head into the unknown, which makes us vulnerable. It makes us uncomfortable.

But outside of our comfort zone is where we really grow and develop because that is where the truth lies. That is where the real opportunities lie. Until we become willing to give up the comfort of, "I know," and the security that we feel in looking good and sounding good, we won't be able to progress to a higher level. Only when we embrace our vulnerability can we access the incredible strength that resides within, beyond the reasoning of our conscious mind.

Most people want to stay in a fixed location where they feel most at ease, be it mentally, emotionally, spiritually or physically. They want to keep the jobs and the relationships that they know, even if those things aren't working well. They want to stay in their childhood church even though they are no longer growing spiritually. They want to continue hanging out with those friends who aren't going anywhere. To drop these people and things means that you may find yourself out there in the world, possibly all by yourself. But that's what it takes: being out there by yourself, walking across the bridge on your own power to make it to the other side.

By definition this is a personal (and sometimes lonely) journey. But that is where faith comes in—during the solitary, uncertain moments of your private walk over the chasm between the known and the unknown. Purpose, happiness and abundance lie on the other side of that bridge. Whatever you are looking for is on the far shore of faith. You'll be able to receive exactly what it is that you're supposed to receive and it's going to be more than you ever imagined. You'll be taken to places that you could never have believed because now you're not trapped in your own mind. You are not trying to direct the show. You're allowing life to take you in the direction that you're meant to go versus trying to figure it all out, guessing and second-guessing what it takes to have an extraordinary life.

Part of the journey is allowing life to unfold, rather than forcing or manipulating things into happening on your schedule. Let Spirit move through you as you cross the bridge. Your practice of mindfulness and self-awareness will help you to be at peace even when circumstances make it appear that there's no way forward, that the bridge is unstable beneath your feet. You must be able to relax even when doors close that you believe should have remained open. In this life you will undoubtedly face setbacks and letdowns. When your back is against the wall, this process may not only feel uncomfortable, but downright impossible. But it can be done, if you refuse to allow your circumstances to predict or define your outcomes.

Transformation sometimes requires that you give things up. You may have to give up people or ideas that block you from going forward. Remaining open to the process, even when it looks like you're losing what's important along the way, will help shift your consciousness to a higher level. That's when your eyes open up. The blockages begin to dissolve.

Depending on material things to enhance your wellbeing—
the idea that you need a job or certain amount of money—are
major blocks to your emotional and spiritual evolution. These
ideas stop you from getting to the truth of where you need
to go.

This is a letting go process: giving up ideas, opinions,
judgments, criticisms and letting God direct your path. The
psalmist says in chapter 23: 2b, "He leads me in the path of
righteousness for His namesake." (NKJV) I can't say what it
means to be "led on the path of righteousness" because it's
such a deep and personal spiritual truth for each individual.
But I can say that the path of righteousness is also the path
of right thinking, right action, right activities, right housing,
right employment and right communication. Whatever is
meant for you to experience on your journey will come to you
when and where and how you need to experience it.

I believe that God provides for us in all ways and, as
Luke12:32 records Jesus saying, "It is the Father's good
pleasure to give you the kingdom." (NKJV) It is His pleasure
to give us our heart's desire. This will be demonstrated as we
allow Spirit to transform us. Our attention gradually moves
away from "I know" and focuses on spiritual principles such
as surrender, acceptance and allowing. This is the most direct
path to becoming truly unstoppable. The things that would
stop you—the negative beliefs, fears, doubts or setbacks that
would normally leave you feeling discouraged—lose their
power.

Crossing the bridge from reason to faith is the only way to experience this transformation. You can try to maneuver around the bridge or swim the river beneath it but it won't work. We must all cross the bridge. Many people take this idea and try to tie it to dogma or to religiosity. They say, "There is only one path to God and it's my religion or my belief system and everyone else is wrong!" But in a deeper spiritual sense, what we're talking about is walking the bridge from reason to faith. It's not about, "I worship the right way and you worship the wrong way, therefore I am on the one true path and you're not." We're not talking about religiosity or tradition. This is about becoming present to the truth about who you are as a child of God; it's about declaring the truth of where you want to go and what you want to have happen in your life. This is the path of faith. It allows us to see that there's much more out there than what we're dealing with in our material world.

I was a person who was committed to intellectual pursuit. I was compelled to study and attain multiple degrees. I wanted to prove people wrong about me. I wanted them to know that I was smart. I could learn. I could grow to be somebody important. I wanted to drop the labels that I had been given as a child. And I had to go on this same journey as well, becoming present to my intellectual might. Doing inventories of my life and looking at all the work that I put into growing and becoming better helped me embrace this path of faith. I looked at all the challenges that I faced, which ultimately led me to a state of surrender. I gave up fighting.

Being shot in the head was ultimately a spiritual experience that took away my fear of death and gave me a moment of direct communion with the spirit of God. Things got much clearer after that. Distractions no longer held weight with me. I was freed up to choose again and I chose the path that would lead me across the bridge. That doesn't mean that I didn't argue with myself along the way, because I did. Sometimes I didn't want to do the things that I was being directed to do. I didn't believe that the changes that I'd prayed about were actually happening.

Moreover, walking this path doesn't mean that there won't be any obstacles. Rest assured, there will be plenty of obstacles. But what changes are the ways that you handle the obstacles that arise; you begin to rely on your faith and your vision rather than solely relying on your reason and your own might.

I have held onto the vision for my life that I've been shown over the years and it still continues to pull me in the right direction. I was willing to change my entire life in order to answer that call. My willingness brought me three thousand miles across the country and put me in the right positions to actually do the work. So crossing the bridge brought me clarity. It also brought greater self- compassion. Over time, when I would run into obstacles in my path I found that I was no longer tempted to break down or revert back to old patterns and behaviors. I had to trust in knowing that my needs were met, the table was prepared. Goodness and mercy would follow me all the days of my life. No good thing would God withhold from me.

I learned how to talk to myself lovingly, reinforcing the good that had already happened and was continuing to happen. I would remind myself consistently that there's a greater good and a greater call awaiting me. It's my job to allow it to show up in my life as I continue to look to the hills from which cometh my help. I realize my help comes from the Lord.

We must each identify for ourselves where our help comes from. Then you lean on that source. I can say that your help comes from the Lord, but until you recognize that truth for yourself the words will hold no weight. You must know for yourself and lean into your knowing. Yield to it. When you yield to a power greater than yourself it takes the stress, anxiety and work away from the business of life. This is how people are able to live in joy despite dire circumstances. Being part of something greater allows them to be incredibly productive. The things that they do may not look or feel like "work" because they're living in joy and purpose. They have answered their call.

You can answer your call in any number of ways. You can answer the call through struggle and hardship and pain and heartache. Or you can answer that call willingly and with joy, freedom, openheartedness and acceptance. You then become a catalyst to change the lives of others so that we can all eventually live our best and greatest lives. This is how we all become unstoppable.

At our spiritual core, we are all unstoppable. We are divine emanations of the creator, here by design to demonstrate God's perfect will in our lives. We're here for one another. From this space we see life differently. Everything can shift. Our finances can shift. Our health can shift. Our relationships can shift. Our whole attitude about life can shift if we allow these principles to manifest themselves within us fearlessly and stay the course. We become beneficial to ourselves, the people of our communities and all those who will come after us. We're building a future for them, each in our own individual way.

None of us are here to walk the exact same path or to believe exactly what someone else believes. Each of us has a distinctly individual call and no one else can duplicate your calling. No one can do what you do the way that you do it. So we are here to accept ourselves as we are. We're here to open our hearts, our minds and our spirits to receive what we've already been given by Divine appointment. We must each do our share. And though we all contribute in different ways, we're all moving toward the same purpose—to become unstoppable.

Reflections

I related to...

_____

_____

_____

_____

_____

_____

_____

_____

_____

_____

_____

_____

_____

_____

Printed in the United States
By Bookmasters